ORANGE CRUSHED

ORANGE CRUSHED

A SEASON ON THE BRINK
at America's Biggest Football School

DARREN EPPS

ISBN 0-97189-749-2
Library of Congress Catalog Card Number: 2006921093

Editing by Henry Oehmig and Arlene Prunkl
Book Design by Fiona Raven

First Printing July 2006
Printed in Canada

Published by Jefferson Press

jefferson press

P.O. Box 115
Lookout Mountain, TN 37350

To God, my co-author,

To my parents, who thought making $20,000 a year to write sports was a great opportunity,

And to my brother Matt, who let me write game stories about beating him in 1-on-1 basketball before he beat me up.

Contents

Introduction

As HURRICANE-WEARY Louisiana natives vigorously waved the red, white and blue flag of New Orleans and embraced fellow LSU season ticket holders they had waited an anxious twenty-three extra days to see; and as millions more gathered around televisions to watch a football game instead of radar screens, signaling a return to normalcy after the fury of Hurricane Katrina, a different type of revival took place inside Tiger Stadium on September 26, 2005.

The brief revival of three Tennessee football careers.

Gerald Riggs Jr., the expressionless running back attempting to redefine a tumultuous career at Tennessee, took a handoff from Rick Clausen on Tennessee's first possession of overtime.

He needed just one yard to reach the end zone, change his legacy and complete one of the most stunning and unlikely comebacks in school history. LSU linebacker Cameron Vaughn met Riggs at the goal line and wrapped his burly arms around the senior's chest, just above his No. 21.

Riggs was trying to make a comeback of his own.

Regarded as one of the nation's top running backs coming out of Red Bank High School in Chattanooga, Tenn., and the son of former NFL star Gerald Riggs, the 6-foot, 217-pound senior toiled as a backup for more than two seasons. He spent more time in Tennessee coach Phillip Fulmer's office, it seemed, than on the field. He missed class. He showed up late to meetings and even walk-throughs. He exasperated the coaches, who called him lazy and immature. Riggs' grades were so poor his freshman season the Southeastern Conference ruled him academically ineligible for the Peach Bowl. He had failed to pass six hours of class.

College life didn't start much better on the field. Riggs' relationship with then-running backs coach Woody McCorvey deteriorated so much that Riggs considered transferring following an uneventful sophomore season. Through two years, one of the most highly recruited running backs in the country had just 256 rushing yards and one career touchdown. Against Duke.

"There's always been a deal about my maturity, or lack of maturity," Riggs said. "I think that was blown way out of proportion. Not to make any excuses, but the expectations that I had coming into Tennessee were pretty high, and, for a lot of reasons—injuries and my relationships with certain people—I didn't really get that going as early as people would like to see it. People got frustrated because of all of the hype surrounding me coming in."

One person at Tennessee believed—a hyperactive, high-fiving, bouncy new assistant coach who wore his hat backward and called each of the running backs "Taylor" to match his own last name because he considered them family. Riggs said he struggled dealing with all the hype, and the perception of him was false. Trooper Taylor had never heard of Riggs. Fulmer and offensive coordinator Randy Sanders wanted to make Taylor aware of Riggs' attitude problems, but Taylor, the newly hired running backs coach, asked them to let him make his own judgment.

Riggs had a fresh start. It was as though he had transferred without ever leaving Knoxville.

"He had started questioning his own confidence and his own ability," Taylor said. "If you tell somebody he's sorry long enough, that's what he's going to be."

In addition to coach McCorvey's heated criticism, Fulmer often blistered Riggs in the media early in his career, taking shots at his pass-blocking ability and refusing to compliment the embattled tailback. Brag on him once, Fulmer believed, and Riggs would feel content. You had to constantly push him. You had to constantly scold him. You had to constantly remind him he could be better.

All Riggs wanted was a coach who would listen to him. Taylor opened his office, his home and his ears to Riggs, who often spent hours with the thirty-five-year-old coach discussing life, family, girls and, of course, football.

In Riggs' junior season, Taylor's first year, he averaged fewer than 15 carries per game and still rushed for 1,107 yards. In Tennessee's shocking win at Georgia, Riggs filled in for an injured Cedric Houston and rushed for 102 yards against one of the nation's top run defenses. In the SEC championship game against undefeated Auburn, which had allowed just one rushing touchdown in 12 games, Riggs carried 11 times for 182 yards and scored twice, including an 80-yard sprint to tie the game 21–21 in the third quarter. Riggs took the handoff, burst through a gaping hole on the left side and left several Auburn defenders and a career full of disappointments behind him.

"Look, he deserved some of the scrutiny," Taylor said. "He deserved it by his actions and his decision making. You can't control what people say about you. What you can control is your own decisions and the way you respond to adversity. He didn't do a good job of that. He went into the tank rather than fighting his way out. I told him, 'Anybody can get knocked out. The guys that get up are the ones who are special. I can find a busload of guys that will lie down and just take it.' I think he scrapped."

With Vaughn trying to pull him away from the goal line as fans screamed on a muggy night in Baton Rouge, Riggs scrapped. He pumped his legs furiously, overpowered the 237-pound Vaughn and willed his way into the end zone. Game over. Tennessee 30, LSU 27. In his third career game as Tennessee's primary tailback following two lackluster performances, Riggs stood defiantly in the purple and gold end zone. He had arrived.

It was his last significant run of the season.

Rick Clausen jogged toward the Tennessee huddle to resounding boos from the LSU fans, the same people who had cheered for the quarterback three years before, with the Vols trailing 21–0 in the second quarter following a disastrous interception thrown by Erik Ainge. Clausen was, of course, beaming as he approached his stunned teammates. "Why the long faces?" he asked with a smile. "We're about to go down here and score."

Just days before Clausen trotted onto the familiar LSU turf with a grin and an unwavering attitude, he had nearly ended his college football career. Talk about a long face. Furious when Fulmer stripped him of the starting job after he threw just five passes the previous week against Florida, Clausen cursed at his coach during a meeting in his Neyland-Thompson Sports Center office and threatened to pack the belongings in his Knoxville condo and move back to California, where he could mentor his younger brother and highly rated quarterback prospect, Jimmy Clausen. Only a phone call from his parents encouraging him to play out his senior season kept Clausen on the practice field the week of the LSU game.

Fulmer's quick hook symbolized the frustrating, seemingly doomed career of the outgoing Clausen. He spent two years at LSU, started one game against Ole Miss and was promptly told by then-coach Nick Saban he wasn't good enough to play for the Tigers. Most quarterbacks take the hint and transfer to Division I-AA schools, where they can play immediately, earn the starting job, post PlayStation-like numbers and become a star on campus.

Clausen rarely takes a hint. Not only did he want to continue playing Division I football, he wanted to remain in the SEC, the nation's toughest conference, and start at Tennessee just like his older brother, Casey. Never mind that Clausen already had one chance to start at LSU and completed a measly 5-of-12 passes for 35 yards and an interception as a redshirt freshman. Never mind that recruiting services projected him the third-best quarterback out of the three Clausen brothers. Never mind that the NCAA attempted to curb transferring within the conference by forcing players to sit out two seasons unless their coach granted them a release. Clausen needed Saban, the meticulous, stern, unyielding coach, to release him to an SEC school to avoid sitting out two years. It's an almost unheard of practice in the SEC. A nightmarish scenario for any coach is to release a player to another conference school, watch that player develop under a rival team and then come back to haunt you.

Saban, who left following the 2004 season, and LSU didn't exactly anticipate being haunted by a skinny quarterback with little potential and even less arm strength. Saban considered Clausen's proposal, shrugged and released his third-string quarterback to Tennessee, where he became, yet again, a third-string quarterback.

Clausen's experience in Knoxville was even more maddening. He lost his chance to start before the 2004 season even began to two freshmen, Ainge and Brent Schaeffer, who were posing for prom pictures just three months before. Clausen had put his life into this game, throwing footballs with Casey as a little boy (when they weren't skidding across lakes on one ski, which both could do in their preteen years) and studying tape provided by his father, who coached football at high schools and small colleges in California. Now, these two kids, Ainge and Schaeffer, who couldn't find the geology building with a map and a tour guide, had him back on the bench. It was August, and the coaches were already asking Clausen to tutor the eighteen-year-old quarterbacks.

Take a hint.

But Clausen hadn't transferred to Tennessee in hopes of carrying a clipboard for two players who couldn't even go out to the clubs with him after a game. He studied game tape each week as if he was going to play. He treated every pass in practice like it was fourth-and-10 in the national championship game. And when Ainge went down with a shoulder injury just one week after Schaeffer broke his collarbone, Clausen took over and went 3–1 as a starter. At the Cotton Bowl against Texas A&M, the kid who had not been good enough to play at two SEC schools held the Offensive MVP trophy after throwing for 222 yards and three touchdowns in a 38–7 win.

His father was ecstatic. "This one is for every kid who was maybe a little too slow, didn't have the arm strength and all those other things," an emotional Jim Clausen said after the game. "He's a great kid. I told Phillip when he wanted to transfer that I didn't know if he could play here or not, but he's a heck of a kid. I'm a little choked up. He's just handled it so well, probably a lot better than I would have handled it."

The glow didn't last long. Even after Clausen outplayed Ainge the following spring practice, even after he clearly beat the sophomore out during fall camp, even after he threw for more touchdowns and fewer interceptions in UT's scrimmages, Fulmer named Ainge the starter on August 27 in a season the Vols expected to play for a national championship. Privately, teammates questioned the decision and only one receiver, Robert Meachem, made himself available for interviews following the announcement. The rest disappeared. Clausen tried to escape, but sports information director Bud Ford implored him to make a statement to the media. Clausen approached the reporters and cameras, offered a short, terse statement, wheeled around and headed out the door nervously playing with his cell phone.

"It's making a decision off of what you think can best get you to the Rose Bowl or get you to the championship game," Fulmer said.

But Ainge looked awful in the second half of a surprisingly close win over the University of Alabama-Birmingham, and Clausen earned the start against Florida. He threw just five passes in the 16–7 loss and lost his job. This time, Fulmer said, for good.

"It's not working out," said the coach.

Take a hint.

Back in Tiger Stadium, Clausen stood on the turf where he didn't belong, in front of fans who had grumbled over his one start against Ole Miss and near an opponent's sideline where he was unwanted. Down 21–0 in the second quarter, Clausen threw a touchdown pass and ran for another as he led the greatest comeback in Tiger Stadium history. As Riggs stood defiantly after scoring the game-winning touchdown, Clausen picked up the football and heaved it into the LSU student section.

"I just wanted to say, 'Thanks for all the good times, thanks for harping on me and writing articles like you did while I was there saying I wasn't good enough to play there,'" Clausen said.

It was his last significant throw of the season.

The wince was gone. For two quarters during the LSU game, ESPN cameras seemed to delight in showing Fulmer's trademark wince—lips pressed, eyes closed, head tilted back and face scrunched. Ainge's fumble. Ainge's "bridal bouquet" toss out of the end zone. Riggs' fumble. All three had triggered the wince. During his twelve-year tenure as head coach, Fulmer had ample opportunities to perfect the facial expression. He winced when Georgia's David Greene hit Verron Haynes in the end zone with six seconds left to beat Tennessee in 2001. He winced for about two weeks after the Vols fell to LSU in the SEC title game that year, a loss Fulmer calls the hardest of his career, and winced every time he looked at the scoreboard when Georgia beat UT 41–14 in 2003. But his wince following Tennessee's Cotton Bowl victory over Texas A&M was much different.

It lasted the entire off-season. The spring was supposed to be an exciting prelude to the season whenever Fulmer saw all those returning starters in Tennessee's lineup. Too bad he was distracted by the mental images of different lineups—those involving some of his players and the Knoxville police. Two weeks after Tennessee crushed Texas A&M in the Cotton Bowl, defensive tackle Tony McDaniel punched a fellow student in a pickup basketball game with such ferocity it broke four bones in his face. Less than a week before UT started fall camp, a video of the incident became public and anyone with a computer and access to the Internet could watch McDaniel deliver the blow and, along with some of his teammates, walk away as the student, Edward Goodrich, lay motionless under the basket. One person, later described as a football player, dribbled up to the victim, peered down at him and then dribbled away.

Less than two months later, Daniel Brooks—already nicknamed "D-Block" by his teammates because, as one former teammate said, "that's where he'll spend the rest of his life"—was implicated in yet another fight but wasn't charged. One month later, receiver Bret Smith and quarterback Brent Schaeffer were arrested for their roles in a fight. Two days later, defensive end Robert Ayers and linebacker Jerod Mayo turned themselves into authorities and faced simple assault charges stemming from the same brawl involving Brooks. Four fights, four months. Spring practice wasn't even over yet.

Following the Ayers/Mayo incident—Mayo was later cleared—Fulmer addressed the media with a red face, shaky voice and, of course, a wince.

"It's disturbing, particularly in light that we have a chance to have a really good team," Fulmer said. "Our efforts need to be centered toward trying to win all of our games rather than on who's in court this week."

The UT beat writers agreed Fulmer had never looked so angry in a public setting. Privately, though, Fulmer had been equally distressed over his own personal issues. Alabama lawyer Tommy Gallion, convinced that Fulmer had helped the NCAA put the University of Alabama on probation, attempted to subpoena Fulmer, drag him into court and, many times, resorted to name-calling. Former Alabama recruit and UT player Kenny Smith also sued Fulmer for defamation. Court documents from the Logan Young case, which sought to prove Young used money to steer talented Memphis prep defensive tackle Albert Means to Alabama, published Fulmer's cell phone number publicly, and it swiftly circulated the Internet. Fulmer received numerous harassing phone calls and quickly changed the cell number many high school coaches around the nation knew so well.

"Legal battles went on and there were even some threats of harm to some of the people involved and their families—including mine," Fulmer said. "I do not take that lightly, and I am not over that yet as far as being angry about that."

An unusually verbose Fulmer, fresh off defending himself and his program during his opening statements at SEC Media Days, spoke candidly of his team's chances to win a national championship. He compared Ainge to Peyton Manning. He even bragged about Riggs. "I think we can have a very good football team," Fulmer said with a smile.

But the wince soon returned. In their first conference game, the Vols looked horrific in a loss to Florida. So much for a national championship. In their second conference game, they trailed 21–0 at halftime to LSU. So much for an SEC championship. It was only September.

But Fulmer implored his team to keep fighting, Clausen caught fire, the LSU defense grew weary and quarterback JaMarcus Russell threw a critical interception. And, suddenly, Riggs fought his way into the end zone, and a huge grin replaced Fulmer's wince.

"I don't know if there has ever been a better story than Rick Clausen," Fulmer said. "I really don't, in all of college football. He's a tough-minded guy. He obviously had to handle the disappointment at the beginning of the week, and he handled it with toughness and class. His teammates rallied around him. Getting done what he got done was unbelievable."

Fulmer, though, wasn't aware that his wince would return many times over the next few months. As he gushed about Clausen's performance on national television, the quarterback stared straight ahead and never looked at the blue eyes of his coach. Moments after one of the most memorable wins in UT history, tension mounted between coach and player for a national television audience to witness.

Like LSU's revival inside a steamy Tiger Stadium that night, the Tennessee Volunteers' revival in 2005 was also short-lived.

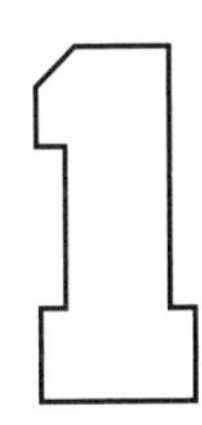

Great Expectations

No reporter covering any portion of Phillip Fulmer's first twelve full seasons as Tennessee's head coach could recall the normally unpretentious fifty-five-year-old so confident, both publicly and privately, in his football team.

Fulmer's personality has always resembled his offense—conservative, rarely flashy and normally effective. Fulmer might bore reporters with his answers and keep the pages of their notebooks blank, but he makes very few headlines with his comments and keeps expectations minimal considering all the hype and pressure. In Knoxville, a slow-developing city with a small-town feel and a population of 173,000, representatives from three daily newspapers, two Internet sites, three TV stations and two radio stations—one with three daily UT-related talk shows—converge on Tennessee's campus for practice, and it isn't basketball.

There's an insatiable demand for Knoxville's plethora of media outlets, too. For six Saturdays every fall, almost 110,000 orange-clad fans—increasing Knoxville's population by about sixty-three percent—descend on old, historic Neyland Stadium in the heart of UT's campus and alongside the Tennessee River, the only river on earth that flows in all cardinal directions. And so do the fans. They come from cities like Chattanooga, Nashville and Atlanta, some on ritzy yachts as part of the Vol Navy, and some in massive RVs decked out with satellite televisions and top-shelf liquors. The men typically wear orange polo shirts with a small, white *T* embroidered on the chest, while the women sport orange tank tops, adorned with a flashy pin featuring the Tennessee logo. And they are obsessed with Tennessee athletics. Even Tennessee's men's basketball team, which boasts almost no tradition or history, plays in a 25,000-seat arena. More than 20,000 fans will even attend the occasional women's basketball game. Directions to a Tennessee sporting event will almost always include Todd Helton Drive, Peyton Manning Pass, Pat Head Summitt Street, Chamique Holdsclaw Drive, Johnny Majors Drive, Tee Martin Drive or, of course, Phillip Fulmer Way just outside Neyland Stadium. Knoxville's area code is 8-6-5, which spells "V-O-L."

Tennessee's supporters also come from one of the 113 cities in Tennessee with populations of 1,000 or less, many of which are located in the Appalachian Mountains. They clinch bottles of Bud Light and wear faded orange shirts, some commemorating the Vols' 1998 national championship. Together, these people, from big cities and small mountain towns, rich and poor, drunk and sober, join as one to watch an event bigger than any Tennessee Titans game, louder than a NASCAR race in Bristol and more popular than deer hunting. A Tennessee football game isn't the only event in the state. It's just the most important. Only two other colleges in the country, Michigan and Penn State, boast higher attendance figures.

Much later in 2005, when the Vols began to struggle, receiver Jayson Swain said, "Football runs deep here. That's probably one reason a lot of us came here. Everybody cares so much. The students, the faculty, the fans, everybody. You can sense it every time you walk across campus. People will look at you, then turn their heads when you look at them."

While the previous descriptions of Tennessee fans are, of course, stereotypes, there remains one distinguishing truth that unifies all of the Volunteer faithful: their expectations are astronomical. And no matter how different these orange-clad fans are from Sunday to Friday, they all share a common belief on Saturdays: the Vols should win. If not, someone should be fired, the program is in shambles, and the sun, in fact, may not rise tomorrow. Perhaps the deep-rooted belief that Tennessee should win every game developed slowly over time. From 1989 to 2004, a span of sixteen seasons, the Vols never won fewer than eight games and went to a bowl game every year, the third-longest streak in the nation. Perhaps their expectations grew from 1995 to '98, when the Vols compiled an astounding 45–5 record and stymied Florida's run of conference championships by winning the SEC title twice. Or perhaps fans started basing success on national championships when Tennessee won the first Bowl Championship Series national title with a 23–16 win over Florida State following the 1998 season.

Before the 2005 season, one of the members on Tennessee's numerous Internet message boards asked fellow posters—the most cynical and hardened of UT's supporters—to predict the Vols' final record. These aren't the lovable fans who worship Fulmer, but they aren't the fans who skip a Tennessee football game to attend a friend's wedding, either. They consider themselves part of the Tennessee family, and no one knows that better than right guard Cody Douglas.

Immersed in a game of PlayStation at his friend's house in Knoxville on January 17, 2005, Douglas refused to answer his ringing cell phone. It rang again. He ignored it. It rang again. He looked away. Several more times Douglas' cell phone lit up without any answer. Each call made him more nervous. Good news rarely comes in a barrage of phone calls from home. Douglas wanted to pretend his family was fine. He tried to focus on the video game.

Finally, a text message forced him to make a call that would change his life forever. "You really need to call your mom," the message read.

Douglas' older brother, mentor and father figure, Zack Douglas, a sheriff's deputy in Galveston County who had just earned his master's degree in health care administration, was dead after crashing his all-terrain vehicle near his home in Texas. He was thirty-two. "When my mom told me, it felt like somebody just hit me," Douglas said. "All I remember is stumbling about twenty yards and hitting the floor."

Douglas also fell hard in his personal life. For two weeks, he refused to leave his home near Houston and return to class at Tennessee. What was the point? He played football for his brother. He had dealt with the agonizing pain in his left foot in 2004 to stay on the field and make him proud, even though he wasn't playing well.

During spring practice in 2005, Douglas' foot still ached, and his brother was gone. He didn't want to play football anymore.

Douglas remained on the ground.

Linebacker Kevin Simon and Tennessee's family of message-board posters were there to pick him up.

Simon wears a tattoo of his brother's face on his bicep and carries a picture of Ken Simon, shot and killed in a Sacramento restaurant in 2001, on every Vol Walk. He changed his jersey number from No. 5 to No. 2 in 2005 to honor his brother, who wore the same number in high school. Simon's father, like Zack Douglas, is a beloved fixture on the Big Orange Nation, a Rivals.com message board devoted to UT football. Cy Simon's posts are often detailed, insightful, opinionated and witty.

Cy Simon called Cody Douglas' home. Look at the message board your brother always checked, he said. Sure enough, post after post swamped the message board with offers of thoughts and prayers to Cody. Many of the members sent cards and flowers.

Using his brother's screen name, Douglas posted a reply that, in part, read, "We received calls, flowers and cards from Vol fans all over the country expressing their heartfelt sympathy to our family. It's comforting to know that I have a huge second family that I can lean on in tough times, and it reassures me as to why Zack and I chose UT as the place I would go to college."

But like any family, Tennessee's most passionate fans expect a lot from their team. So out of the 361 members who participated in the poll to guess the Vols' final record, 71 picked the Vols to finish undefeated, despite road games against Florida, LSU, Alabama and Notre Dame, the subsequent SEC title game and a likely match-up against Southern Cal in the Rose Bowl. Almost two hundred more picked Tennessee to finish with just one loss. Two members predicted seven wins, the lowest total of any response.

And no matter what the reasons are for their expectations, fan reaction following a Tennessee loss is equally predictable. Fans will blister the team, coaches and players on WNML radio well into the night, some slurring their words, all astonished their beloved Vols could actually lose.

"Having ten wins, not many people will fuss at that," Fulmer said during the 2004 season. "But we fuss at it here."

The biggest football school in America also boasts, for better or worse, the biggest expectations. After one particular loss, the language turned so foul on Brent Hubbs' volquest.com message board that he posted a reminder concerning the rules about abusive rants toward players and coaches. The subject heading of Hubbs' post was, "All right, here we go..."

It was the Vols' second loss of the season. They were still nationally ranked.

Fulmer's take? "It's part of the passion, part of the level of interest and the coverage. There's so much coverage nowadays that everybody thinks they have an opinion, which, if they buy a ticket, they do, I guess. They're entitled to it," he said.

The hysteria around them rarely distracts the players, impressive for a batch of eighteen- to twenty-two-year-old kids. Tennessee's players seemingly always exit their weekly Monday meetings with Fulmer feeling they are underrated no matter what expectations the fans might have. And Fulmer's humbling tactics, when applied with any merit, often work. The Vols won three straight road games as double-digit underdogs, beating Florida in 2001, Miami in 2003 and Georgia in 2004. But Fulmer, in Lou Holtz fashion, can invent ways to make every opponent the favorite, despite what Vegas lines may predict. Members of Tennessee's defense felt slighted against Louisiana Tech in 2004 due to the hype surrounding star running back Ryan Moats. If Tennessee played the Little Sisters of the Poor, the Vols would somehow feel like underdogs because they had less experience.

Fulmer could also convince the media. Tennessee played in the SEC championship game four times in eight years from 1997 to 2004, but started the season ranked in the top five just twice. In 1998, one season after winning the SEC title, the Vols started tenth and won the national championship. And there was Fulmer, downplaying his team's ability and using phrases like "we're a million miles away" the entire journey.

Until 2005.

No one, not even Fulmer, could resist discussing Tennessee's enormous potential following the 2004 season. Eighteen starters on a team that played undefeated Auburn close in the SEC championship game and then throttled Texas A&M 38–7 in the Cotton Bowl would be back in Knoxville. When star defensive back Jason Allen surprisingly said he would spurn the NFL and return for his senior season, the Vols had ten of their eleven starters on defense back from a 10–3 team.

Allen's startling announcement in January of 2005, considered a crucial step for Tennessee to win a national championship, befit his personality. Allen is an extremely intelligent twenty-two-year-old who earned his high school diploma and college degree in less than seven years. A slight lisp accompanies his confident way of speaking, though he isn't a brash loudmouth like other outspoken players of his caliber. He just likes attention. Allen followed the media's coverage of Tennessee closely, and he loved seeing his name in the newspaper. Tennessee officials attempted to curb player access starting in 2004 by allowing only a few players to speak on Mondays and Wednesdays to go along with Tuesday's weekly media day. But they couldn't restrict Allen. Though his teammates often begrudgingly attended these sessions or skipped them altogether, Allen was a staple during Monday's abbreviated media opportunity, and he never missed Tuesday's media day. He also offered to participate in every Wednesday teleconference for opposing teams' writers. (After Allen suffered a season-ending hip injury in 2005, reporters bemoaned a media day without the effervescent star. But Allen showed up anyway on crutches even though no one requested his appearance.) At SEC Media Days in July of 2005, Allen sported a flashy pinstriped suit and extravagant blue, black and white-colored shoes.

So when Allen pulled out a wrinkled piece of notebook paper during a press conference to supposedly announce his intentions to enter the NFL draft, members of the media knew they were in for a show. His story played out like a movie. Allen said he decided to enter the NFL draft earlier in the week following a visit with his parents at their home in Muscle Shoals, Ala. He even interviewed agents and narrowed his list down to three. On the drive back to Knoxville, Allen began to reconsider his decision to turn pro. When he arrived at his condo to start packing up his clothes, Allen said he found a small sheet of paper in one of his dresser drawers. The crumpled note listed his goals for the 2004 season. He called his mother, Cynthia, and said, "I reviewed my goal list, and there were things that I had not accomplished. If I do not accomplish them, I would be cheating myself. I'm not the type of person who's going to give up. I set these goals, and I didn't reach them."

After reading from his list of goals, Allen described a dramatic moment as he informed family members and coaches of his decision to remain in school. Everyone marveled at the power of Allen's little note, fans ate the story up and his mother cried at the press conference. Quite a production.

There was more to the story.

Allen wanted to play cornerback. He spent most of the 2004

season at free safety to fill a need, leading the SEC in tackles and likely becoming a second-round selection in the draft. But Allen knew that 6-foot-2, 202-pound safeties, such as himself, with good speed are pretty standard in the NFL. Allen, however, had great speed, clocking a 4.4-second time in the forty-yard dash. And cornerbacks with his size and speed become first-round picks who earn millions and millions of dollars. At a meeting in Muscle Shoals, Allen told Fulmer and defensive coordinator John Chavis he wanted to play cornerback. Fulmer and Chavis, surely dousing their star with praise, told Allen they needed him more than ever before at free safety. Robert Boulware, Corey Campbell and Jarod Parrish all failed at strong safety the previous year, and undersized, 5'8" Jonathan Hefney was the only candidate to replace Allen at free safety, the most physical position in the secondary.

Allen upped the ante, telling Fulmer and Chavis he would return to Tennessee on one condition: he would play cornerback. Fulmer and Chavis weren't about to tell a returning co-captain, one of the conference's best players and a future NFL star, thanks but no thanks, you go enjoy pro football.

No wonder Allen wants to be an agent once his playing days are over. He managed to heap attention on himself, win over the fans with his rich story, boost his draft stock *and* play cornerback.

He's good. And Tennessee's potential to win a championship provided Allen an even greater forum to showcase his abilities. ESPN televised one of Tennessee's practices. Numerous magazines proclaimed the Vols as national championship contenders and several predicted them to play Southern Cal in the Rose Bowl. USC and Texas were the obvious picks to win the national title; Tennessee was the sexy pick. The SEC media overwhelmingly picked Tennessee to win the conference. The names of several Vols appeared on pre-season All-America and All-SEC lists. The first AP and coaches' polls ranked the Vols third, their highest pre-season ranking since 1999 and their highest ranking in any poll since December 2, 2001, the day after they stunned Florida in The Swamp.

"I plan on having at least a couple of rings after 2005," Allen had said at his press conference.

Fulmer quietly felt the same way about his teams in 1998, 1999 and 2001. But 2005, in so many ways, was different.

For the first time in his coaching career, Fulmer publicized those thoughts loudly and often. The more media, the better. Later in the season, Fulmer explained why he suddenly sounded more like Steve Spurrier than Lou Holtz. He was trying to avoid a situation like the one Auburn endured in 2004, when the Tigers went undefeated but started too far back in the pre-season poll to catch USC or Oklahoma. Fulmer transformed from college football coach to promoter. "I was trying to do the political things when being third behind USC and Texas and trying to position ourselves," he said.

Fulmer's campaign trail started in Knoxville, where he told the local media at a summer breakfast he thought the Vols would be "special." He continued to Hoover, Ala., for SEC Media Days, where he publicized those feelings in front of five hundred media members from all over the country. Reporters accustomed to engaging in games of Solitaire on their computers as Fulmer lumbered through the Tennessee depth chart suddenly whipped out the blue SEC notebooks placed at each chair. Fulmer wasn't simply listing hometowns and statistics; he was talking about the players on Tennessee's often-criticized offense. He started by comparing sophomore quarterback Erik Ainge, who started all of six games as a freshman, with Peyton Manning, an NFL MVP, former Tennessee great and school record holder in almost every passing category. Listen to Fulmer, and you start to think UT was already finding a street to dub Erik Ainge Drive.

"I think Erik has a lot of the same qualities that Peyton Manning had when he came in as a freshman and sophomore," Fulmer said. "I am very encouraged about his future. Our wide receiver group as a whole should be one of the best in the league. Our offensive line, well, I expect it to be as good as we've had at Tennessee."

No one blamed Fulmer for elevating Tennessee's goals so high. No one warned him about increasing the lofty expectations of fans. No one discouraged him from boasting to the media. Why should they? The Vols had more talent, more experience and more depth than any Fulmer team since 1999. The Vols' offensive line featured four upperclassmen—all NFL prospects—and a tackle, Arron Sears, who the coaches said could be the best in school history. Fulmer said he could use ten different linemen in a game by midseason and still feel comfortable. Tennessee's top five receivers would be number one options at most SEC schools, particularly sophomore star Robert Meachem, who led the Vols in receiving yards and yards per catch as a redshirt freshman in 2004. But if anyone on this wildly-confident football team knew how to remain humble and motivated, it was Meachem.

Meachem, a baby-faced, admitted people-pleaser with a peculiar sense of humor, grew up on a small farm outside of Tulsa, Okla., with a football, a basketball and a rope. That's right, a rope. Meachem's father's side of the family is all cowboys and calf ropers, and his grandfather, Emory Metcalf, was the oldest black cowboy in the state of Oklahoma.

"I still love the rodeo," Meachem said. "If I had a choice between becoming a pro football player or a top professional rodeo rider, that would be a tough decision."

But Meachem's life has been a wild, bumpy ride, and not because he spent it riding bulls. At the age of twelve, his childhood horse, Little Man, was stolen. His parents divorced, and their small farm fell on hard financial times. Days after Fulmer called him the most advanced freshman receiver he'd ever coached, Meachem suffered a season-ending knee injury and redshirted in 2003.

And then there's the story of Meachem's sister, Tammie Terrell Brown, a chronic asthmatic who died at the age of twenty-three. Doctors told Meachem's mother, Beverly, that Brown wouldn't live past age eight. After she turned eight, it was twelve. After twelve, it was sixteen. After Brown prevailed through her illness—even giving birth to a child—the family stopped listening to the doctors. Meachem saw his sister go on life support nine times and watched as shock treatment brought her back to life on four occasions. A skin disease triggered by the asthma caused her to shed dead skin and left sores on her entire body. She sometimes had to walk on the sides of her feet.

And yet she persisted through her health problems until her death at the age of twenty-three, when Meachem was thirteen. Her words ring in Meachem's ears during games, meetings, classes and just before he goes to sleep.

"If you ever get a chance," she would say, "show the world what you can do."

Following his sister's wish, Meachem and Ainge torched SEC defenses as freshmen. Imagine what they could do with a year of experience. It would be like playing catch in the backyard.

"I don't know that since I've been coordinator, I've had a year where I felt like I've had as many pieces to the puzzle in place," said offensive coordinator Randy Sanders, a witty, outgoing, born-and bred Tennessean who ran Fulmer's offense but was hardly similar to the head coach. Reporters often joked that five minutes in the Neyland-Thompson Sports Center media room, where the forty-year-old Sanders leaned on a folding table and answered questions far longer than any other assistant coach, would generate at least two notes for the daily notebook. During these sessions, Sanders came across as funny, honest, direct, and typically humble. Such is the personality of someone who had been a career third-string quarterback at Tennessee back in the mid-1980s.

"In 1999, we had an awfully good team returning that had a

lot of experience. I think we're probably better now in the offensive line. We're better and deeper at tight end than we were then. We don't have near the depth at running back, and we're similar at receiver, but we're maybe more explosive there right now. As a group of five receivers, they're probably as good as any we've ever had or we've had in a long, long time."

And the offense was still considered the team's weakness. The strength of Tennessee's team was on defense and, in particular, the front seven. Tennessee's defensive line included Hawaiian Jesse Mahelona, who earned All-America honors in 2004, Cotton Bowl Defensive MVP Justin Harrell and Parys Haralson, an intense, vicious All-SEC defensive end who had gained notoriety for hitting quarterbacks after the whistle but wore glasses and always said "yes, sir" and "no, sir" off the field. Fulmer also said tackle Turk McBride "might be our best defensive player." And he was a backup.

Leading the defense was the toughest competitor of them all, defensive coordinator John Chavis. Nicknamed "Chief," Chavis speaks in a low, gruff tone and rarely smiles in front of reporters. During his Tuesday media session, Chavis often looks at the watch on his left wrist in between questions and once ordered a reporter out of his sight because of a comment he heard the journalist make on the radio.

Broach the right subject, and Chavis is eloquent. He'll speak at length of his loyalty to Fulmer, who promoted Chavis in 1995—then a virtually unknown linebacker's coach—to defensive coordinator against the wishes of many Tennessee fans. He'll also boast about the types of people on his defense, including

Haralson, who donates much of his spare time to the Boys and Girls Clubs of America.

But Chavis rarely singles out individuals. Ask about Mahelona, and you'll hear about all the defensive tackles. Ask about Simon's return from an injury, and you'll hear about all the Vols who play hurt. Single someone out, Chavis says, and another player will feel slighted. Comparing players was out of the question. Discussing Tennessee's deep pool of defensive talent, however, was too stirring for Chavis to resist a rare show of excitement.

"I think we have more people we can put in the game than maybe at any other time I can think of," Chavis said. "There's not a dropoff. We've got some people who can play. I don't like to compare, but maybe even more than 1999. We're ahead of where we were last year. Talent-wise, there's no comparison."

Listen to the coaches, and you start thinking Tennessee might win Super Bowl XL. The media, locally and nationally, was also guilty. Now, the players, the same ones who had felt challenged by Louisiana Tech a year ago, were starting to display their own excitement. They discussed their national championship aspirations freely and even developed a motto that found its way onto orange T-shirts: "One Heartbeat."

"We could be better than any team Tennessee ever had," linebacker Jason Mitchell explained, "if we play as one."

They played for the first time in a scrimmage setting on Saturday, August 13 inside Neyland Stadium. Lightning and thunderstorms quickly moved the scrimmage indoors, but the results didn't change with the scenery. Tennessee's offense, a serious concern in recent years and the major question facing the Vols entering 2005, blistered a stout and highly touted defense indoors and outdoors. The result stunned and embarrassed members of Tennessee's defense, gave the much-maligned offense a tremendous boost of confidence and brought a smile to the face of Fulmer. Under Chavis, the defense would be fine. The offense constantly worried Fulmer, a former offensive lineman who spent most of his time in quarterback, receiver and linemen meetings and on the offensive side of the field during practice ever since Tennessee's 8–5 season in 2002.

Fulmer didn't want to leave the offense on this rainy Saturday. And not because he was counting mistakes.

"There were some big plays on offense, which I was glad to see," he said. "It's night and day from this time last year with the quarterback position and being able to do a lot more things."

Following the scrimmage, Ainge glanced through the open door of the Neyland-Thompson Sports Complex at Haslam Field, rolled his eyes and shook his head. Exactly one year ago, Ainge had endured one of the most difficult moments of his career during his first collegiate scrimmage on Tennessee's outdoor practice field. He completed 3-of-14 passes for thirty yards as the offense turned the ball over five times and scored just once. "Oh, man," Ainge said, smiling as he reflected back on his first scrimmage. "Everything was going a hundred miles per hour. You're just kind of looking and throwing and getting guys blown up. You really can't compare it to now."

Sanders said he was equally impressed with how well the

two quarterbacks managed the offense. Clausen and Ainge interpreted all of the hand signals from the sideline without any problems, neither one used wristbands, and there were no miscommunications. In 2004, Sanders called twenty-five to thirty percent of the offense in the first scrimmage. On this Saturday, he used about eighty percent of the playbook. "Where we were then and where we are now," Ainge said, "are two completely different offenses."

The offense's performance was even more impressive considering veteran receivers Chris Hannon, Robert Meachem and Jayson Swain were limited due to injuries. Freshman Josh Briscoe caught six passes for ninety-nine yards and Lucas Taylor, another freshman, caught four passes for ninety-five yards and hauled in a sixty-nine-yard touchdown pass.

"If we're completing a lot of balls to Josh Briscoe and Lucas Taylor," Ainge said, "then just imagine when those other guys are all healthy."

Imagine the lanky Meachem tracking down another Ainge bomb. Imagine speedster Chris Hannon outrunning a defensive back toward the end zone. Imagine C.J. Fayton sprinting away from the defense like he did in the Cotton Bowl. Ainge did, and Fulmer couldn't help himself, either. The smile under the straw hat he wore during fall camp became a regular part of his post-practice interview sessions. He complimented his team frequently. His chuckles almost outnumbered the questions concerning Tennessee's quarterback competition.

Fulmer, as several reporters pointed out to him following

Tennessee's final Friday practice before game week, was in a good mood. Again.

"Well, I am pleased," Fulmer said. "I've got an experienced group of guys that really play hard. If you're good on defense—and I think we're going to be really good on defense—you feel good. I coached defense for three years. I know if you're good there you've got a chance to have a winning team. We got through camp without injuries, we've got quarterbacks and some young, talented guys. So, yeah, I'm real happy."

As he began to walk toward his car so he could go home and help his wife prepare a dinner for Tennessee's freshmen and sophomores, Fulmer suddenly stopped and turned around.

"I'm glad y'all think I'm feeling good," Fulmer said with another chuckle. "That makes me feel better."

Fulmer felt at ease. Members of the defense felt at ease. Ainge felt at ease. Sure, the quarterback situation didn't resolve itself in fall practice, and the Vols never could duplicate their explosive performance in the first scrimmage. So what? They had been competing against a dominant defense who could carry them to the Rose Bowl. No worries.

"All you've got to do on offense when you have the defense we're going to have is don't turn the ball over, score 28–35 points per game and you won't lose," Ainge said.

It sounded so easy. Especially with one of the nation's winningest coaches more motivated than ever to win.

Coach Phillip Fulmer:

The Unadorned Dean of SEC Football

IT IS LIKELY Phillip Fulmer will never be fully embraced by Tennessee fans.

Unless he can add to his current legacy another national championship or two and, say, fifteen more years of success in the program, he will never be an icon like Joe Paterno, Bobby Bowden or Tom Osborne. He will also have tremendous difficulty matching the expansive popularity of Mark Richt, Urban Meyer or Pete Carroll. And he will probably never earn the national recognition of Bob Stoops, Nick Saban or Steve Spurrier. Fulmer actually owns a better winning percentage than Spurrier and the same number of national titles (one), but who would most fans rather have coach their team?

Only five other coaches in the history of college football—Osborne, Barry Switzer, Bud Wilkinson, George Woodruff and Amos Alonzo Stagg—won a hundred games more quickly than Fulmer. And the latter two were around before helmets and forward passes. Entering 2005, Fulmer boasted a 101–25 record over the last ten years, a better mark than anyone in the SEC, and the best winning percentage (.799) of any coach with at least ten years of experience. He had a ridiculous streak of fifty-four straight weeks in the top ten. Tennessee entered the 2005 season as champions of the unforgiving SEC East four times in the last eight years. Alabama fans would be mortified to know that Fulmer, if he coaches ten more years as he says he will, should pass Bear Bryant on the all-time SEC wins list (and he's beaten Alabama nine of the last eleven times, giving more credence to Tide fans' disdain for him).

Fulmer, in short, ranks among the very best college football coaches nationally, though you will not usually hear his name in that discussion. No one is naming their first-born son after Fulmer or hanging pictures of him reverently in their house. Fans typically like Fulmer. But they don't *adore* him. It's a curious paradigm, and the reasons are numerous and not always fair to the fifty-five-year-old from Winchester, Tenn.

Unlike Meyer, Richt and Stoops, Fulmer is not a sleek, youthful-looking coach. He's an old offensive guard, and he looks like one. He's hefty and balding and aging quickly—a comparison of his current look to his picture in 1998 is startling—and he's forced to wear bright orange quite frequently. Not even Brad Pitt could pull off the orange gear Fulmer wears to practice and on the sideline during games.

Fulmer's personality is equally unappealing to fans who want to see their coach exchanging laughs with the boys on ESPN's "Pardon the Interruption" like basketball coach Bruce Pearl. Fulmer doesn't have a wild temper like Paterno, a lovable catch phrase like Bowden's "*Dadgum* it!" or a commanding presence like Meyer and Stoops (particularly Meyer, who can bring a room to a standstill). No one calls home and exclaims, "Did you hear what Fulmer said?" as they do with Spurrier, who did a hilarious impression of pitcher Kenny Rogers to a cameraman on—where else?—a golf course. Fulmer doesn't play much golf. And he doesn't wear a visor. He wears a simple baseball cap and invites his children on the sideline with him during games.

Other reasons for Tennessee fans' tempered admiration of Fulmer:

- He's awful in bowl games: the off-season in college football is eight agonizing months. Some pregnancies don't last that long. That's a lot of time to ponder the season's final game. In the case of Tennessee fans, that's a lot of time to be festering negative thoughts toward Fulmer. In 2003, No. 6 Tennessee lost by thirteen to unranked Clemson in the Peach Bowl. The previous year, an unheralded Maryland team blew out Tennessee 30–3. The Vols lost by two touchdowns in the 2001 Cotton Bowl and got embarrassed 42–17 in the 1998 Orange Bowl by Nebraska.
- His national championship is tainted by the tremendous

amount of luck needed to win it: Florida couldn't master the art of kicking a short field goal in Tennessee's 20–17 overtime win in Knoxville; Arkansas quarterback Clint Stoerner inexplicably fumbled as Tennessee fans headed for the exits in the Vols' miraculous 28–24 win; and, in the national title game, an injury to star Chris Weinke forced Florida State to start Marcus Outzen at quarterback. Dadgum it, indeed.

- Spurrier owns him: It's hard to become a legend when one of your conference rivals—division rivals—absolutely owns you. Fulmer is 3–7 against Spurrier, the dashing former Heisman Trophy winner. The losses mount on his legacy and his mind.

"Oh, it's terrible," his wife, Vicky Fulmer, has remarked. "It might even be worse as the years have gone by. He does not like to lose. After a loss, he becomes extremely withdrawn. If you try to talk to him, he doesn't even hear you."

But no rationale outweighs the one Fulmer will never be able to shed. The main reason Tennessee fans aren't stirred to put grandbabies in their laps to talk about Coach Fulmer is because he waltzed into one of the great situations in college football history. Tennessee was already an established program—a dominant program—before Fulmer took over full-time in 1993. In the four previous seasons prior to Fulmer's promotion to head coach, the Vols won 38 games and two SEC championships under Johnny Majors. In 1989, Majors took an unranked Tennessee team and guided it to an 11–1 finish and top-ten national ranking. The following year, Tennessee won the Sugar Bowl.

Fulmer didn't exactly resurrect a dormant program. UT fans weren't desperate for a coach riding a white horse into Knoxville to save them. Fulmer simply picked up where Majors had left off, winning ten games per season and the occasional SEC title with a ho-hum, run-oriented offense while Spurrier's Gators smashed passing records and threw the ball all over the field to the delight of college football fans not wearing bright orange.

But on July 29, 2004, during SEC Media Days in Hoover, Alabama, Fulmer showed a side of himself never before seen by Tennessee fans or almost anyone in college football. He used words like "absurd and frivolous" to describe the actions of Alabama-based lawyer Tommy Gallion, who tried to prove Fulmer had conspired with the NCAA to bring down the Crimson Tide program. He spoke in a raised voice. He showed a sense of humor. He even addressed his weight problem.

And UT fans *loved* it.

The voice, laced with that Tennessee accent unmistakable to Volunteer fans, was familiar.

The tone was not.

No knob on the tiny black speakerphone commanding so much attention in Hoover could alter the voice's sharp pitch. Fulmer, the typically conservative, often dry coach who rarely made headlines with his words, unleashed a tirade at SEC Media Days from the safety of Knoxville mostly aimed at Gallion, without ever mentioning him by name.

"A small group of radical attorneys, on their own, have undertaken their own agenda to smear the NCAA and anyone else they can along the way," Fulmer said, reading from a statement. "These irresponsible people have alleged there was a conspiracy between the Justice Department of the United States, the FBI, the NCAA, the University of Tennessee, and me. These kinds of statements are absurd.

"They make wild charges, incredible exaggerations and tell half-truths to try and make their case. The truth is not on their side. I simply do not intend to play their game."

Gallion had sent a letter to SEC commissioner Mike Slive promising not to disrupt Media Days after Fulmer announced he was skipping the event. "If you believe that," Fulmer said, "I've got some oceanfront property in Arizona I want to sell you."

The room, filled with five hundred media members, roared with laughter. But they weren't safe, either. Fulmer took a shot at them.

"A couple of you called me a coward. I was disappointed to see that," Fulmer said, referring to local columnists. "You can talk about my coaching if we lose. You can talk about my play-calling in games. You might talk about my physique if you choose to stoop that low, but coward is way over the line."

Fulmer was rolling now.

"You'd be upset, too," he said, stunning reporters with a furious tone in his voice. "I had to really work at letting this not be a distraction to me in going and doing my job, and it really hasn't been up until now. It's so frivolous and stupid. I'm working on it not being a distraction. But, yes, I am very upset about it. But we'll get through it."

Fulmer's approval rating among Tennessee fans soared to the levels of 1998. Their coach, battered by Gallion and his crew for years, was fighting back. He was calling their actions absurd. Did he use the word "stupid?" He sure did. Man, he was pissed. But at least he defended himself. At least he showed a personality. He's one of *us*, UT fans reasoned. He said all the things they had been posting on message boards for years.

And a funny thing happened to Fulmer following his late-July outburst. He ditched his conservative style of thinking. It was as if the momentum of unleashing a tirade at SEC Media Days made him a new coach. Three weeks later, he named two freshmen, Brent Schaeffer and Erik Ainge, co-starting quarterbacks. This is the same coach who started Mark Levine at tailback at Florida in 1997 instead of a back named Jamal Lewis, who had the unfortunate distinction of being a freshman. Now, Fulmer was starting two freshmen quarterbacks? Schaeffer would be the first SEC quarterback in fifty-nine years to start his first game straight out of high school.

The following month, Fulmer started riding around the foothills of the Smoky Mountains in a 2005 Harley-Davidson Softail Fatboy given to him as a surprise by his wife, Vicky, and his three daughters for his fifty-fourth birthday.

"It's a great stress reliever for him," Courtney Fulmer, the oldest of Phillip and Vicky's three daughters, told *The Tennessean*. "He'll take off on rides, and you know his mind is racing."

The next spring, Steve Spurrier, the new coach at South Carolina, referenced Tennessee's off-the-field problems in Columbia's

The State newspaper. Fulmer, who typically took Spurrier's verbal jabs like a winded fighter, fired right back the following day.

"He needs to take care of his own house and leave mine to me, first of all," Fulmer said. "He's got plenty of issues over there I'm sure to deal with. We've had a lot worse things than this that we've gotten through. I don't give a crap one way or the other what anybody says except the people that count."

The reaction stunned Spurrier. This was a new Fulmer.

"Phil said that?" Spurrier asked the reporters who informed him of Fulmer's comments.

The new, hardened, I-don't-give-a-crap Fulmer was back. Former offensive lineman Bubba Miller, who occasionally dropped by practice, joked that Fulmer was mellowing out in his old age. But this was the old Fulmer. This was the Fulmer that went 33–5 during a Spurrier-like run from 1997–99.

"To be honest, we weren't crazy about Phil Fulmer," Miller said. "I know a lot of guys don't necessarily have a love affair with the coach. But there were times where we would get tense because he was a mean son of a bitch. He could be. And you hated him at times. But there was never a Saturday when we went out there that we didn't feel like we were primed to kick somebody's ass."

On every fall Saturday in 2005, Fulmer was going to be primed to do just that. He felt it. He *knew* it. Almost every player in the starting lineup during the rout of Texas A&M in the Cotton Bowl was back. The Vols were absolutely loaded. This was going to be the mid-1990s all over again. And Fulmer wasn't afraid to tell anyone. In the old days, he kept quiet about Tennessee's expectations. But SEC Media Days had changed him. And exactly one year later, this time speaking at Media Days in person, Fulmer compared his sophomore quarterback to Peyton Manning and didn't hesitate to discuss his team's chances of winning the Rose Bowl.

If this new Fulmer, the outspoken, brash head coach with a better winning percentage than anyone with ten years of experience could follow through and actually win a second national championship, his legacy would forever change.

"I just want to be remembered as one of those guys that got to the top, stayed at the top and is always knocking on that door," Fulmer said. "And then, opening it enough times."

Fulmer said he'll likely tire of beating down the door before he reaches the age of longtime coaches such as Paterno and Bowden. But he's still got ten more years left in him.

Long enough to catch Bear Bryant.

It'd be a legacy, years from now, some aging East Tennesseans could tell their grandkids about. As it turned out, everyone would remember 2005 for Fulmer's colossal mishandling of a fairly important position on the field.

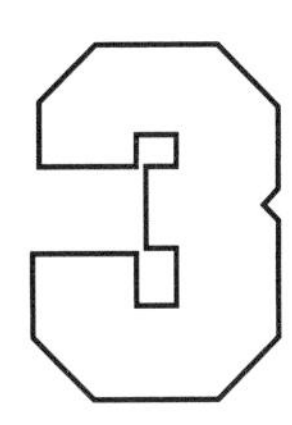

Coin-Tossing for Quarterback

THE COURSE OF RECENT Tennessee football history at the quarterback position changed on two baffling, mindless, completely unrelated plays—one on October 5, 2002, and the other on November 6, 2004—though no one inside Neyland Stadium realized their significance at the time.

And certainly no one fathomed the strain both plays would put on the 2005 season.

Understanding the importance of the first play requires a little creativity. Leading 17–10 at home late in a game against Arkansas in 2002, Tennessee defensive back Julian Battle sprinted toward quarterback Matt Jones, who was scrambling in his own end zone after a UT punt pinned the Razorbacks at the 8-yard line.

Normally, Battle's bold dash would go unnoticed among fans. He typically played safety, but a flurry of injuries on the 2002 team forced Battle to play cornerback at times.

This was one of those times. So as Battle bolted toward the quarterback, apparently forgetting he was playing cornerback, almost everyone in the stadium—including Jones—saw bewildered Arkansas receiver Richard Smith running by himself down the right sideline. No one was within 40 yards of him. And Battle never got to Jones.

It was a 92-yard touchdown pass that sent the game spiraling into an epic six overtimes, finally culminating in a 41–38 Tennessee win.

"Just a blown assignment," Battle said with a shrug following the game.

And a blown chance at landing prep quarterback phenom Chris Leak, who set a national high school record by throwing 185 touchdown passes at Independence High School in Charlotte, N.C.

In one of the overtimes following Battle's "blown assignment," Arkansas linebacker Tony Bua drilled Clausen as he released a pass, fracturing his left collarbone.

Long story short: an injured Clausen couldn't play the following Saturday against Georgia and Leak's older brother, C.J., started instead but struggled in two series and was benched for James Banks. Chris Leak, who was expected to sign with Tennessee, wrote an ESPN.com diary slamming the UT coaches for not giving his brother a chance and called Fulmer a liar. A furious Fulmer ended his recruitment of the prep star.

Chris Leak went to Florida.

All because Julian Battle forgot he was playing cornerback.

Without Leak, the Vols scrambled to find a quarterback for the 2004 class and landed Erik Ainge, who took part in a play even more mind-numbing than a cornerback forgetting to cover a receiver. Leading 10–7 against Notre Dame on a mild November afternoon in Knoxville, the Vols took over at their own 30-yard line with forty-two seconds left in the half following a punt. Take a knee, and go into halftime winning a late-season nonconference showdown before finishing off the SEC East title.

Instead, the Vols called a draw play for Cedric Houston, who rushed for two yards to the 32. Fine. The draw play didn't work, the play clock was off and now the Vols could head to the locker room with a three-point lead.

Not yet.

What happened next is still a mystery among players and coaches. Fulmer claims he told offensive coordinator Randy Sanders to call another draw play and run the clock out. As the clock continued to tick, the players looked completely bewildered.

"They said on the sideline if we gain some good yardage on the draw play, we'll get back on the ball," center Chuck Prugh said. "If it's not as successful, we'll huddle up. I think there was some confusion. We looked over and didn't know what was going on."

Neither did the coaches. Sanders said he immediately signaled for a Hail Mary, which was news to Fulmer. "We throw it deep," Sanders said. "If it works, we score. If not, it's incomplete, and that's the worst thing that happens."

Wrong. Here's an even worse scenario: Prugh, a backup center filling in for the injured Jason Respert, snaps the ball low and hits Ainge in the shin. Ainge chases after the ball, scoops it up—by this time, the Neyland Stadium horn is about to sound—and gets drilled by Notre Dame linebacker Brandon Hoyte, who made his intentions quite clear after the game.

"In this game, you don't hit someone just to knock them down, you hit them like you don't want them to get back up," Hoyte said. "And I mean no disrespect by that."

As the Tennessee band prepared to take the field—perhaps if the Stanford band had been on the field, the play would have worked—Ainge was on his back in serious pain near the 20-yard line, a full 80 yards from the end zone. The tissue between Ainge's collarbone and shoulder was seriously damaged, and he wouldn't take a snap the rest of the year.

The Vols didn't even have to run another play.

"I'd like to have that one back," Fulmer said. "You know, ninety-nine times out of a hundred I'll run the football there and run the clock out. It's my responsibility. It was a low snap. Erik is a competitor, trying to make a play, and we end up losing a good player. I shouldn't have done that. We should have run the clock out. We should have fallen on the ball. Chuck should have made a better snap. It's bad luck for that to happen.

"It was a mess, just a mess."

Not for a feeble-armed, unheralded, third-string quarterback named Rick Clausen. The broken play signaled the opportunity of his career. He was better known as former UT quarterback

Casey Clausen's younger brother, who couldn't make it at LSU and couldn't throw a Nerf football 50 yards. Since freshman quarterback Brent Schaeffer was also injured, Clausen was responsible for finishing off Tennessee's run to the SEC East title.

And then a funny thing happened. Clausen, prepared to signal in plays from the sideline for the rest of his forgettable career, immediately started throwing touchdown passes. Lots of them. Though Tennessee went on to lose the Notre Dame game—a meaningless contest other than the Ainge injury—Clausen led the Vols to close, shootout wins over Vanderbilt and Kentucky to clinch the SEC title. He threw two touchdown passes in Tennessee's 38–33 win over the Commodores. He threw for 349 yards and two touchdowns in a 37–31 victory against Kentucky.

The players loved Clausen because he spread the ball around to different receivers and was more accurate than Ainge. The coaches loved him because he knew the scheme so well and rarely made poor decisions.

Despite a poor performance against Auburn in the SEC title game, Clausen left the coaching staff no choice but to name him a co-starter in 2005 following the Cotton Bowl. He threw for 222 yards and three touchdowns to earn Offensive MVP honors in a 38–7 blowout of Texas A&M, thrusting himself into the quarterback competition as Ainge watched from the sideline. If Ainge hadn't been hurt, no one would ever have known Rick Clausen was capable of winning football games in the SEC. Instead, Clausen and Ainge were co-starting quarterbacks entering spring practice and in fall camp.

All because Sanders wanted to try completing a 68-yard touchdown pass as time expired in the first half.

And that's how we got to the quarterback mess of 2005.

Dubbed co-starters following an uneventful spring practice, the competition between Ainge and Clausen didn't seem like much of a competition before fall camp. Ainge was the Peyton Manning clone—Fulmer made the comparison himself—who worked at the highly regarded Manning Passing Academy over the summer. He was the freshman UT record holder for touchdown passes. He was the tall, good-looking nephew of former Boston Celtics star Danny Ainge with a cannon for a right arm and a stunning blonde on his left arm. Shoot, the guy even threw passes without looking at the receiver.

"I'm going to tell you a secret about Ainge," receiver Robert Meachem said. "His uncle played basketball, and Ainge played point guard in basketball, right? Well, Ainge can throw a no-look pass in football. Nobody knows it, but he can look over there to his left and throw it back to his right and hit you right in stride without even looking."

Erik's father, Doug Ainge, initially didn't want his son playing football. Too rough, he said. Besides, Erik was already a star in basketball and baseball entering middle school in Glencoe, Ore. But Danny Ainge convinced Doug, his brother, to persuade his son to play football after getting the results of a brain typing evaluation developed by Boston Celtics consultant Jon Niednagel. Based on a video of Ainge answering questions about his life, playing basketball with his older sister and throwing three innings of baseball, Niednagel identified Ainge as ESTP. An ESTP type is a very aware, sensing, dominant right-brain athlete with outstanding visual awareness and superior agility. In other words, the perfect quarterback.

Other ESTP types are some of the best quarterbacks to ever play the game, such as Joe Montana, John Elway, Joe Namath, Dan Marino and Johnny Unitas.

Yeah, Rick Clausen, the balding, feeble-armed, humble, sixth-year quarterback was going to unseat the Big Man on Campus with the famous last name and a brain like Joe Montana. Clausen had a better chance of threading a pass between two defenders on a 50-yard post route. The coaches said Ainge would compete with Clausen for the starting job. Almost everyone knew Fulmer and Sanders, being political, wanted to give Clausen a fair chance in his final year of college and let Ainge beat him on the field.

Only he didn't. The competition, as expected, wasn't even close. But no one figured it would be Clausen completely outperforming Ainge in almost every aspect of the game. This was Buster Douglas pummeling Mike Tyson. This was Villanova shooting seventy-eight percent in the second half to beat Georgetown.

The latter is probably the most accurate comparison, since Clausen completed a stunning 77.3 percent (34-of-44) of his passes in Tennessee's three fall scrimmages for 430 yards and three touchdowns. He only threw one interception. Ainge was 30-of-56 (53.6 percent) for 352 yards, two touchdowns and two interceptions.

Who's the Peyton Manning clone, now?

"Rick certainly seems to be in command right now, and Erik seems to be pressing a little bit out there," Fulmer said.

The quarterback comparison for the three scrimmages looked like this:

Scrimmage 1

No.	Name	Comp.-Att.-Yds.-TD-INT
16	Rick Clausen	10-13-159-2-0
10	Erik Ainge	11-17-129-1-0

Scrimmage 2

No.	Name	Comp.-Att.-Yds.-TD-INT
16	Rick Clausen	10-15-180-1-1
10	Erik Ainge	10-20-91-1-1

Scrimmage 3

No.	Name	Comp.-Att.-Yds.-TD-INT
16	Rick Clausen	14-16-91-0-0
10	Erik Ainge	9-19-132-0-1

Following Tennessee's second scrimmage, Clausen was the clear leader. "Rick did real good. He calmed down and had fun out there," Meachem said. "I think if Ainge calms down and has fun like Rick, we'd have two great quarterbacks."

Ouch. Not only was Clausen winning the quarterback competition on the field, he was winning over his teammates off the field. It's an old football cliché: If you have two quarterbacks, you really have none. The University of Texas rotated Major Applewhite and Chris Simms with little success and lots of controversy. Mark Richt's rotation of senior David Greene and junior D.J. Shockley didn't even produce an SEC East title on a team stocked with NFL talent.

"It divides the team," Doug Ainge would later say. "It just splits everybody. It splits the players, the coaching staff, the fans, the parents and the media. Everyone has an opinion on who should start. It's not good for teams. I'm a coach. Believe me. How often does it work?"

Only in this case, the players didn't seem so divided. They gravitated away from the confident Ainge toward the humble Clausen, one of the most popular players on the team. It was easy to see why Clausen was so well-liked. Ask Clausen about himself, and he'd give you the standard, coach-speak answer, then heap all the credit on his teammates. Ask Clausen about one of his teammates, and he'd launch into a compliment-laden discourse that could easily fill a reporter's notebook. Clausen could make a scout-team player sound like an All-American.

Ainge, contrary to his growing reputation as an ego-maniac, wasn't a bad guy or the next Kelley Washington, the boastful former Tennessee receiver who once said the coaches "get paid the big money" to get him the ball. Ainge just behaved like most nineteen-year-old quarterbacks would if compared to the NFL's MVP, boasting a touch of arrogance, and he lacked the personable traits Clausen displayed. Clausen even befriended Ainge, a rarity between two competitive athletes vying for a high-profile position.

But Clausen was friends with seemingly everyone on the team. He was the opposite of his older brother Casey, a reclusive quarterback who hadn't meshed well with a group of young receivers as a senior.

"Rick's really cool. If we're in the club, Casey pretty much would sit in the corner," receiver Chris Hannon said, "but Rick's dancing. He'll dance. He'll go ahead and get down. He's a real fun guy to be around. That's one of the guys on the team I could be around all day."

Just like he did on the dance floor, Clausen often urged his receivers to hang out with him in the meeting room. They watched extra film together. He threw extra balls to them after practice to get their timing down. He even took them out to eat wings, giving each receiver an opportunity to voice his expectations for the season.

"Rick goes and asks us if we want to go in the film room," Hannon said. "Everybody watches film together."

Even Fulmer took notice. "Rick has a personality that's a real plus for him, and he can kind of rally the troops," Fulmer said. "They'll spend the extra time with him in the film room. He's a popular guy off the field."

Fulmer's practice evaluations were the one place Clausen lacked popularity. No matter what the stat sheet read after each scrimmage, Fulmer couldn't resist Ainge's potential. Every now and then, between getting intercepted and taking a sack, Ainge would hit a receiver in stride on a 30-yard crossing route between two defenders. Or loft a jump ball beautifully down the sideline. Ainge was also more mobile than Clausen, who might not have been able to outrun all of his linemen. The previous season, Ainge hadn't taken a true sack and, thanks to a background of playing point guard, weaved his way out of trouble on numerous occasions.

But then Ainge would throw a deep pass into triple coverage or launch a no-look pass—not the kind he was throwing during summer drills—just before a defender tried to grab him and stop the play. Fulmer cringed. This was supposed to be easy. Ainge had the rocket arm, the perfect brain type, the nifty moves and Manning on speed dial. Clausen knew the offense pretty well and took the receivers out for wings.

And yet the competition dragged on.

Two weeks before the season opener against UAB, and still no decision: "It's the coaches' decision. Whatever decision they make is fine by me," Clausen said. "I'm not the most gifted guy in the world, but I know the offense."

Ten days before the season opener, and still no decision: "I'm more concerned about who's going to be the third quarterback than I am who's going to be the first or the second," said Fulmer, clearly annoyed with the constant questions about his quarterback situation.

Eight days before the season opener, and still no decision: "I think I've done what I'm capable of doing—spreading the ball around, getting the ball to the athletes and putting the offense in the best place possible," Clausen said. "Whether I've done enough, Coach Fulmer and the coaching staff will decide that.

I'm happy with what I've done, and I'm just waiting for a decision, whatever they say."

Clausen, who downplayed the ongoing controversy, grew uneasy as the co-starter label remained. The longer Fulmer put off making the decision, the lower Clausen's chances of starting sunk. And Clausen, an intelligent veteran at twenty-three years of age, knew it. If Fulmer was basing his decision purely from Ainge and Clausen's performance in fall camp, the choice would have been easy.

But it wasn't easy. The Vols weren't just trying to win the SEC East or earn a BCS bowl bid. They were playing for a national championship, and the college football nation expected them to make a run for the Rose Bowl. A consistent, methodical quarterback like Clausen, Fulmer thought, can beat Vanderbilt and Kentucky. But Clausen had struggled in the SEC title game against Auburn. Could he beat Georgia, Florida and Alabama?

Maybe. But Fulmer knew he had a quarterback who could—one who already did.

Almost a week to the minute before No. 3 Tennessee opened the season against UAB, Fulmer gathered his team in the middle of Haslam Field following the team's annual kicking scrimmage. Ainge sat in the middle of his teammates, his green no-contact jersey obvious among a mass of orange and white.

At the edge of the group was another green jersey. The popular, outgoing Clausen stood off to the side closest to the locker room, his head hanging and his feet fidgeting. Fulmer called the team together to announce a starting quarterback. The scene under gray skies and a slight drizzle gave the answer away. Sanders once joked Ainge and Clausen would arm-wrestle for the starting job. In a way, Sanders wasn't kidding.

Fulmer named Ainge, with a stronger, more dynamic arm, the starting quarterback over Clausen following a meeting with his assistants earlier in the morning. Fulmer said both quarterbacks would play against UAB, though he wasn't sure when Clausen would enter the game. But unlike last year's situation with Ainge and Brent Schaeffer, Fulmer would not call his two quarterbacks co-starters Saturday. Ainge was the quarterback. Clausen would enter the game when necessary.

"Erik will start the game because we think he gives us a little bit more mobility," said Fulmer, who also evaluated the quarterbacks by watching tape of every play during the 2004 season. "He gives us a little bit more arm from the standpoint of being able to throw the ball down the field."

As the rain fell harder, the questions from reporters poured down faster on Fulmer. Wasn't Clausen a co-captain, the favorite among his receivers and linemen?

"It's not anything about politics or liking someone. It's making a decision off of what you think can best get you to the Rose Bowl or get you to the SEC championship game," Fulmer said. "If I were going to try to make a decision off of politics, I'd be running around like a chicken with my head cut off all the time."

Hadn't Clausen completely outperformed Ainge in the scrimmages?

"We've been inserting, and that's not really Erik's forte because he's been here for a limited amount of time," Fulmer said. "Rick has a better understanding of more things. Like I said, Erik's got a little bit more mobility and a little bit better arm.

"Rick did a great job. I don't know how else to say it. It wasn't just one of those clear-cut things at all. You could have gone the other way. You have to look at it like, 'Who's going to handle things the best?' Is Erik going to come off and give you a big play if things aren't going well in the game, or is Rick going to come in and be a calming effect, which I think is the case because he can manage things. It's tough. You could have flipped a coin. I didn't want to do that. I wanted to make a decision off of what was black and white as best I could. I believe that's the right decision. We'll see."

Aren't you worried Ainge will be looking toward the sideline to see if Clausen's warming up every time he makes one of his patented ill-advised decisions?

"I am concerned about that," Fulmer said. "I tried to address that with them this morning—not to look over the shoulder, not to be pressing or trying to do something dynamic. Play within the system. I hope they'll listen to that very well."

The rain fell at a furious pace now on this dreary Saturday, but none of the soaked reporters were moving. The words flowing from Fulmer's mouth and into saturated notebooks were creating more questions than answers. Fulmer said he didn't want to put any pressure on Ainge to make plays, but the quarterback who clearly beat him out would be standing just a few yards away on the sideline ready to take over. Fulmer wouldn't even guarantee

Ainge would start for the entire season, or even the second game. "We'll find out in the first game who's going to be in the second game," Fulmer said.

Talk about pressure. Tennessee's second game of the season was a showdown in Gainesville against No. 10 Florida. Ainge and Clausen were essentially trying out for the right to start in what could be the most important game of the season.

So, to clarify: Ainge was the starter even though Clausen regularly outperformed him, but not really the full-time starter because Clausen would play, and no one was sure when Clausen would play, and no one was sure who would start in the biggest game of the season in three weeks. Oh, and the third-string quarterback would be freshman receiver Lucas Taylor.

Huh? The previous year's rotation between Ainge and Schaeffer to start the season had at least some order and structure. Schaeffer would play the first two series, Ainge would play the next two, and so on. The rotation kept defenses off-balance since Ainge and Schaeffer brought two different styles to the field, kept the two quarterbacks from looking over their shoulders and kept them involved in the game.

This new rotation, as explained by Fulmer, kept everyone confused.

After about twenty minutes, Fulmer was done talking and the group headed indoors, where Clausen and sports information director Bud Ford were engaged in a whispered debate. Clausen, who bottled up his opinion of the quarterback competition during fall camp out of respect for Ainge, finally showed some emotion when Ford approached him about speaking to the media. Clausen refused. Ford, a gray-haired forty-year veteran in the business who ran his department with almost military-like, old-school discipline, implored Clausen to meet with reporters, if only for a few minutes. The normally laid-back, accommodating Clausen still refused.

The two finally made a compromise: Clausen would deliver an improvised statement to the media but wouldn't answer any questions. Clausen walked toward the group of reporters and cameramen, who were standing in one of the Neyland-Thompson Sports Center end zones, and hurriedly spat out his statement.

"Coach Fulmer made his decision," he said. "You've just got to live with it. It is what it is. Basically, that's just the way I'm going to approach it, so, basically that's about it."

He then turned and walked away, nervously playing with his cell phone as he exited the practice facility. An uncomfortable silence fell over the media. Ainge, as expected, stuck around a little longer to discuss Fulmer's decision. And he didn't exactly give himself a glowing recommendation.

"I think it's one of those things where I think it's pretty even," Ainge said. "Coaches have a tendency if it's all even that the younger guy usually plays. By no means have I won the starting position."

His receivers weren't exactly brimming over with praise for him, either. Only one, Meachem, even stuck around to answer questions from reporters following Fulmer's decision. "I think Rick has more experience than Erik right now," Meachem said.

"Rick sees it faster than Erik. But as the game progresses, Erik will get on a roll like he did last year."

One prevailing question remained unanswered. If Fulmer chose Ainge over Clausen because he'd won crucial SEC games the year before, had more mobility and a stronger arm, then why hold a competition in the first place? Everyone knew Ainge had beaten Georgia, Florida and Alabama in 2004. A twelve-year-old sitting in Section ZZ could tell Ainge threw the ball harder and moved around in the pocket better than Clausen.

But Fulmer held a lengthy quarterback competition from spring practice until one week before the season opener and heaped the entire offensive playbook on Ainge, who withered underneath the wealth of information and incredible consistency of Clausen. Now, Ainge's confidence was shaken, Clausen wasn't real pleased and, as Doug Ainge would later say, the competition divided the media, the fans, the players and the coaches. Everyone had an opinion on Tennessee's unsettled quarterback situation.

After practicing from March until August, what was the resolution? Ainge would start, but Clausen would, at some point, still play.

"We've talked through just about every scenario that could come up, I believe," Fulmer said in the rain that fateful Saturday.

He had no idea.

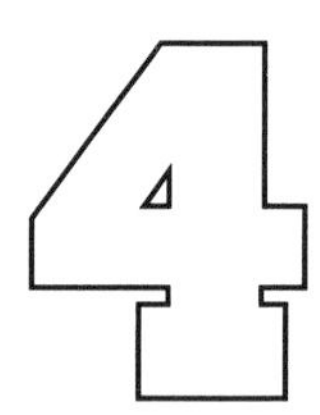

Warning Signs

For months, embarrassed Tennessee fans read about the transgressions of their football team.

They knew that Tony McDaniel had rearranged a fellow student's face during a pickup basketball game, Robert Ayers had destroyed the jaw of a five-foot-eight, 150-pound frat boy, Brent Schaeffer had picked up a baseball bat in a dormitory fight, Bret Smith had punched a student while he was lying on the floor, Corey Campbell had stolen twenty-five feet of coaxial cable from a Wal-Mart and no one was safe around Daniel "D-Block" Brooks.

In all, eleven Tennessee players were arrested or cited for crimes ranging from aggravated assault to underage drinking from February 2004 to April 2005. Four fights involving Tennessee players occurred in a four-month span.

But those problems were over, it seemed; practice for one of the most anticipated seasons was about to begin, and, besides, boys will be boys. Back when Sylvester Croom, head coach at Mississippi State, used play college ball, he said fights broke out among players and students all the time. The police didn't care, the media didn't care, and certainly no one could watch these fights over the Internet when color TV was still considered an innovation. Boys will be boys. College fights, most people thought, were harmless.

That is, until the public saw they weren't, and Tennessee was forced to relive a disastrous off-season all over again. On August 3, two days before Tennessee started football practice, any UT fan with a computer and an Internet connection could watch a sickening, disturbing, violent act involving their talented defensive tackle.

A surveillance video from the University of Tennessee recreation center, released by the district attorney general's office, showed McDaniel, who is six-foot-seven and three hundred pounds, blindsiding student Edward Goodrich with a nasty right hook on January 12 and walking away as fellow basketball players—several of them members of the football team—scattered to the other end of the court. Goodrich remained motionless on his back for a full minute before anyone attempted to aid him.

Goodrich later alleged that some of the football players participating in the pickup basketball game laughed as he lay on the floor. One player walked by him, paused for a moment, and then walked away. Another player gazed down at the motionless young man as he dribbled a basketball, and then he, too, skipped away while bouncing the ball between his legs. After he had remained on the court for a full minute, a student finally attended to Goodrich. Eighteen minutes later, Goodrich finally rose to his feet.

"The way people reacted was the most disturbing part," Goodrich said later.

The punch knocked Goodrich unconscious and broke four bones in his face. The injury required a metal plate to be inserted in his face, and he still experiences numbness in his cheek and around his mouth. Phillip Fulmer suspended McDaniel two games—*two*!—for the incident. "He got off easy," Goodrich said. "To me, it wasn't any punishment at all. It sends a message that football players are above the law. It's all right for him to just hit me and break bones in my face—as long as he can play football."

So while the start of football practice rescued SEC teams from a tumultuous off-season—the multitude of arrests among players in the conference made national headlines—the Volunteers were reliving the experience all over again less than forty-eight hours before the start of practice and the day before players reported to campus.

Privately, some players grew annoyed with the embarrassing headlines and the constant misbehavior of their teammates. Questions about discipline, the state of the program and the chemistry of the team were unavoidable. It was the eve of Tennessee's first practice, the first step toward a national championship, and no one was talking about football.

And so Tony McDaniel closed his eyes and cried in front of his teammates.

McDaniel, along with the other Vols who found themselves in handcuffs during the off-season, stood in front of their teammates during a team meeting and apologized. Typically a shy, quiet, stoic giant, McDaniel broke down in tears as he delivered his apology. He was sorry for causing so much embarrassment, sorry for dragging Tennessee's name through the mud and sorry he contributed to a delinquent off-season. He didn't read from a piece of paper or notecards. He spoke straight from the heart as tears flowed down his cheeks.

"It was emotional," Fulmer said. "I thought that cleared some air. Maybe we can become close through the adversity we've faced."

Said Jason Allen: "We can lay down and say we're going to have a bad season because of this, or we could go down to Atlanta and win the SEC championship. We can bond from this."

Normally, teams bond in response to off-the-field tragedies or close losses on the field. The Vols were going to bond because the team members who beat up people in the off-season were sorry. How's that for a rallying cry? But if the Vols played angry at the world, delighted Fulmer with their practice habits and whipped up on some Gators and Bulldogs, no one would remember they turned the off-season into their personal Ultimate

Fighting Championship. If the Vols didn't show much intensity and looked sloppy in practice, however, it was because they were undisciplined, and all the fights tore apart the fabric of the team.

It was the latter.

Poor practices were the theme of Tennessee's 2005 fall camp. On August 10, Fulmer stopped practice twice and restarted periods because of lackluster play: "If you play seventy plays in a game and you play sixty-eight of them good and two of them not very good, you have a chance to get beat against a good team. That's what I want them to understand."

Two days later, an angrier Fulmer voiced his opinion again: "I think we have a chance to have a pretty darn good football team, but we don't look like it out there. We've got a lot of young guys who don't know how it's done yet. If I knew what it was, I'd fix it. I would have fixed it before it started."

Five days later, the Vols went 0-for-9 passing in the red zone in the afternoon.

"That's horrible," an agitated Fulmer said.

And on August 13, lightning struck, both literally and figuratively.

Tennessee's first scrimmage of fall camp, held inside Neyland Stadium, started with a bang...then another, and another. Thunder sounded in the distance, and lightning could be seen over the northwest corner of the stadium. And on the first play of the first scrimmage, Tennessee's only healthy center, David Ligon, crumpled to the ground clutching his ankle. He suffered a severe high ankle sprain—disheartening news for a three hundred-pound lineman—and would miss all of fall practice and the season opener.

More lightning.

Gerald Riggs Jr., who had carried the ball just three times, wasn't particularly happy about standing on the sideline for most of the scrimmage.

"I'm kind of different," Riggs said. "The coaches kind of like to hold their guys back, especially the guy they're going to be counting on during the season. They don't want to get guys hurt. The more reps I get, the better. As they say, wine gets better with age. I feel like the more I'm in, the more I touch the ball and get in the flow of the game and practicing out there with the first defense and going against them, the more I feel like I'll be ready."

Another running back, David Yancey, couldn't fully enjoy winning the No. 2 job behind Riggs. Fulmer took his scholarship away before the season to make room for a large, highly praised signing class, making Yancey a walk-on once again. "I really don't want to go into details," Yancey said. "That's a real touchy subject. I'd rather not speak on that."

Center Richie Gandy, trying to recover from ACL surgery in the winter—he had torn up his knee playing basketball—partially dislocated his left kneecap when a teammate fell on his leg during live scrimmage drills on August 18. He would also miss the season opener. Now the Vols had no true centers.

Lightning, lightning, lightning.

Not quite the way you would expect a national championship season to start.

Still, Fulmer was in a good mood most days, the Vols were still loaded at almost every position, the practices were getting better, the team was mostly healthy and Rob Smith, normally the starting left guard, was actually playing pretty well at center.

They would be fine, right?

Actually, some of the veteran players weren't convinced Tennessee would cruise to the SEC title. Much later in 2005, defensive end Jason Hall reflected on the pre-season, the arrests, the bad practices and the injuries, and shook his head. "You couldn't help but think, 'Man, something is *wrong* here,'" Hall said.

But the Vols, including Hall, still started the season optimistic about their chances of playing in the Rose Bowl. The tumultuous off-season, the gruesome video involving McDaniel, the suspensions, the bizarre quarterback competition, the twenty-one off-season surgeries, the lazy practices—none of that mattered now. The Vols had a championship to win.

Saturday, September 3 in Knoxville, Tennessee, was the kind of day that made people feel guilty for staying indoors. Unlike Tennessee's first scrimmage, the weather for the first game—a 12:30 p.m. kickoff against twenty-three-point underdog Alabama-Birmingham—was sixty-eight degrees, breezy and without a cloud in the sky. And no one with tickets to the UT-UAB game wanted to be anywhere else.

A noticeable buzz surrounded Neyland Stadium as hordes of

tailgaters excitedly discussed Tennessee's potential by their campers, tents and kegs, and counted down the minutes until kickoff and the official start of another season.

On this day, the orange banners and shirts around the stadium seemed a little brighter, the barbeque smoke smelled richer, the chicken tasted better and the beer went down smoother as fans reacquainted themselves with tailgating partners and other season ticket holders. Not since 1999 had Tennessee fans anticipated a season to this degree, and UAB coach Watson Brown understood why.

"Looking at Tennessee on paper, they're physically the best team we've played in the eleven years I've been here," Brown said. "The only other time we played Tennessee was the year they won the national championship, and I think this team is physically better than that one. I just don't see any weaknesses."

It was, as they say around these parts, football time in Tennessee.

UAB kicks off, and Ainge completes his first two passes to move the Vols into UAB territory. On third-and-4, Ainge throws over the middle and high to tight end Justin Reed, who can't hold on when Marcus Mark levels him in the chest. No problem. James Wilhoit kicks a 46-yard field goal, and the Vols lead 3–0.

On UAB's first play from scrimmage, running back Dan Burks fumbles and Tennessee takes over at the 33. After Riggs carries the ball four straight times, Ainge lofts a majestic fade pass to Chris Hannon on third-and-goal from the 3. Hannon makes a spectacular catch in the corner of the end zone, dragging one foot inbounds for the touchdown. As legendary voice of the Vols John Ward would say, "Give him *six*!" Less than six minutes into the game, and the Vols already lead 10–0.

What day is the Rose Bowl? Where's a good place to stay in Pasadena?

It *was* a perfect day. The 107,529 fans were belting out "Rocky Top" under a cloudless sky, students celebrated in the aisles, players jumped up and down on the sidelines and then, without warning, the music came to a screeching halt.

Fulmer benched Ainge.

"It seemed to Erik and to the Ainge clan, a starter had been named even though there would be some relief pitching later in the game," Doug Ainge would later say. "It wasn't going to be like what was going on with Schaeffer and Erik last year. To me, when you name a starter, it's like saying, 'Go win the game.'"

Tennessee wouldn't be the same again. Not for the rest of the half. Not for the rest of the game.

Not even for the rest of the year.

Clausen, who had stormed out of the Neyland-Thompson Sports Center seven days earlier because he supposedly wasn't part of the quarterback rotation, not only entered the game in the third series following two scoring drives by Ainge, he played all but three snaps in the second half. Ainge, admittedly rattled by the benching, threw an interception on his third pass when he returned to the field in the second quarter. He didn't reenter the game until the fourth quarter when Clausen, who completed 17 of 24 passes for 217 yards, threw an interception.

Following Clausen's pick, the Blazers marched down the field and scored when hefty UAB quarterback Darrell Hackney completed a 27-yard touchdown pass to Reggie Lindsey with 7:50 remaining in the game, cutting Tennessee's lead to 17–10.

Ainge went back into the game—remember when Fulmer said he didn't want his quarterbacks looking over their shoulder every time they made a mistake?—and immediately threw an incompletion while being pressured by UAB's Larry McSwain. On second down, Ainge sailed a pass way over the head of a wide-open Jayson Swain.

On the next play, Ainge misread the coverage and threw a floater intended for Hannon down the sideline. Brandon Register picked off the pass to give the Blazers, 23-point underdogs, a chance to tie the game.

Gulp.

But on fourth-and-7, on UT's eleven yard-line, Hackney zipped a laser through the hands of Lance Rhodes, and the Vols held on for a wildly unimpressive 17–10 win. Ainge was benched three times during the game.

"Everybody's pretty mad," Hannon said. "As players, we thought we'd come in here and beat them by more, but we didn't."

The college football ticker looked like this:

No. 1 USC 63, Hawaii 17
No. 2 Texas 60, Louisiana-Lafayette 3
No. 3 Tennessee 17, UAB 10

Hall was right. Something was wrong.

Especially with Ainge.

On Tennessee's first two drives, Ainge completed three of five passes for 26 yards and a touchdown. After Fulmer benched him, Ainge completed just two of nine passes for 31 yards and threw two interceptions.

"It's just different for me," Ainge said. "The only time I've sat on the sideline my whole life is when I've been hurt. That's why it's different for me. The sooner I can figure that out, the better for the team. Like I said, Coach Fulmer and Coach Sanders get paid the big money to make these decisions. I have complete faith in them."

Tennessee's running game, with a 1,000-yard rusher and four linemen back from 2004, also struggled against a poor UAB defense starting three new linebackers. Riggs rushed for just 48 yards following the first quarter and his longest run went for 15 yards. "There was nothing special from the running game," Fulmer said. "It looked like a bunch of mush at times."

The receivers, who vowed to restore the moniker of "Wide Receiver U" to Teneseee, dropped six passes.

"As you can see," Clausen said, "we've got a lot of things we need to work on."

Two days later, Fulmer was doing his best to make UAB sound like LSU. The Monday following the game, as his players signed autographs to raise money for Hurricane Katrina victims at West Town Mall, Fulmer told reporters he thought UAB would be a middle-of-the-pack SEC team. (UAB would finish dead last in

Conference USA's East Division.) While expressing his discontent concerning his team's play—he called out guards Ramon Foster and Cody Douglas for playing soft—Fulmer noted several times during the off week he thought UAB was a good team. UAB is dangerous, he had warned them before the game.

There. Told you so.

He wasn't telling the players much at all. During the preseason, a few of the UT players, like Hall, thought something might be wrong. Now, they *knew* something was wrong. "Once the coaches started hyping up UAB, we knew something could be messed up," one defensive player said after the season. "Come on, they weren't *that* good."

Perhaps no one is better at self-deception than people involved with sports. Coaches can make any opponent sound like national champions. Players use popular phrases like "wake-up call" and "what we needed" to describe tough games. Fans always believe, no matter how perilous the situation. And the media gobbles it all up and spreads the wrong message to an even larger audience.

Nowhere was this more evident than with the University of Tennessee football team. Fulmer convinced himself that subbing the quarterbacks like a tag-team wrestling event, without order or strategy, would work fine. Three days after the UAB game, Fulmer announced Clausen would start against Florida in Tennessee's biggest game of the year. His declaration that Ainge would be the starter on that rainy Saturday seemed so long ago.

It had only been eleven days.

"Rick will start, and we'll rotate probably like it was," Fulmer said. "I want somebody to take the job and it be it. But my concern is the running game. My concern is consistency. The quarterback is not a concern of mine. I don't think it's a concern of anybody else on this team or this staff."

Self-deception at its finest. Try to convince the receivers, who would later admit they didn't like wondering if the hard-throwing Ainge or the soft-tossing Clausen was going to play. Try telling Ainge his performance wasn't a concern.

He lost his starting job. More importantly, he lost his confidence and couldn't get into a rhythm with Fulmer switching out quarterbacks with reckless abandon.

"It's like a jump shooter," Ainge said. "If you can get in that rhythm and stay in that rhythm, then watch out." Yeah, watch out. Clausen is right behind you.

But it would be okay, Ainge said. He would be fine.

The running game also needed work. If the Vols couldn't dominate the line of scrimmage against UAB, they were in for a long season. "I know personally, for not having the scrimmage time, I think I ran the ball pretty good," Riggs said, taking a veiled shot at the coaches for not working him more during the pre-season. "I was getting my pads low and running hard and breaking tackles. There were just some other things I could have done differently that had nothing to do with time. That's just doing what you're supposed to be doing, and we'll get that fixed."

The running game, Riggs said, would be fine.

The Vols were humbled. The UAB game was a "wake-up call." It's what the Vols "needed" after hearing about how good they were the entire off-season. All those terms that fans, players and coaches use to make themselves believe.

"We've got to get better. We just got to get better, period. That's as simple as it is," Fulmer said. "Potential means you haven't done it yet. I don't know if we were reading our press clippings or what all it was."

It sounded so simple. Even though the offense had struggled for most of the pre-season, had looked awful against one of Conference USA's worst teams and was headed down to The Swamp to take on Urban Meyer's Florida Gators before playing at LSU, they would be fine. They just needed to get better.

The Vols were in denial.

They weren't the only ones.

As the Vols staged their final walk-through at The Swamp, I was picking them to beat Florida. So did veteran beat writer Chris Low of *The Tennessean*. So did almost every member of the *Knoxville News-Sentinel*'s college football picks panel. The sixth-ranked Vols, winners of three straight road games as double-digit underdogs, always managed to pull off an upset when doubt started to creep in. They lost to Auburn by twenty-four points at home in 2004 and then beat No. 3 Georgia in Athens the very next week. They were only six-point underdogs against the Gators.

"I wish we were hundred-point underdogs," UT receiver Jayson Swain said.

It was old school versus new school. It was the dean of SEC coaches (Fulmer) versus the young phenom (Meyer). It was a basic offense (UT) versus the unique spread-option attack (Florida).

"They're not a team that will wow you with scheme," Meyer said. "They are a team that wows you with personnel."

Not on Saturday, September 17.

Fair or not, critics dubbed the Vols an "undisciplined" team following the flurry of arrests in the off-season. On a muggy, uncomfortable night in Gainesville, Florida, the Vols earned that epithet. In a 7–7 game late in the second quarter, Riggs rushed for 16 yards down to the Florida 11. On second down, the Vols were called for a false start. On the next play, Ainge took a three-step drop instead of five steps and missed tight end Chris Brown wide open in the end zone.

"Erik was supposed to take a five-step drop, and he threw it a second too early," Brown said later.

On third-and-13, the Vols made a substitution error and took a delay of game penalty. The Vols had moved the ball to the Florida 9-yard line on second down. Now, they were at the 20. And a mistimed snap on James Wilhoit's 37-yard field goal allowed Florida's Dee Webb to block the attempt. Tennessee wouldn't score for the rest of the game.

There were also special teams errors. Jonathan Hefney fumbled a punt, leading to a Florida field goal and a 10–7 lead. Punter Britton Colquitt, completely ignoring Fulmer's rule of not faking a punt inside the 35, threw an incomplete pass on fourth-and-9 from the 32. The Gators kicked another field goal and led 13–7.

Undisciplined. You could already hear the word tossed around sports talk shows, see it printed in sports sections.

Fulmer once again proved even a head coach with thirteen years of experience could still deceive himself. Fulmer started Clausen, who threw five passes for a grand total of zero yards. Ainge showed flashes of his heralded freshman season, leading the Vols on two long drives in the second quarter. So what did Fulmer do?

Benched him. Clausen reentered the game with 1:13 left in the first half and couldn't even muster a first down.

"We just felt like Rick was a little better in the two-minute situation," Sanders said. "What Florida was doing when we were spread out wasn't easy for the quarterback to manage, especially with the noise and trying to communicate at the line. We thought Rick might be a little better equipped to handle that."

Translation: the Vols had no confidence in Ainge. And predictably, Ainge had no confidence in himself. After Fulmer benched him at the end of the first half, Ainge completed just seven of eighteen passes for 77 yards and no touchdowns the rest of the game.

Before the season started, Sanders had said he couldn't remember coaching an offense with so many pieces in place. Which is why, after two games, Fulmer was so puzzled. A group of five veteran receivers considered among the nation's best couldn't break free against Florida's press coverage. Two proven quarterbacks couldn't take advantage of the man-to-man defense employed by the Gators. A senior-laden offensive line with a senior running back consistently failed to spark any dynamics in the running game.

An offense with all the pieces was in pieces. Tennessee's longest gain against Florida was 19 yards. On twenty-four first-down plays, the Vols gained one yard or less fourteen times. Their quarterbacks were completing just fifty-two percent of their passes.

"Our entire offense is more inconsistent than I thought it would be at this stage," Fulmer said. Tennessee gained 66 total yards and held the ball for just more than ten minutes in the second half and lost, 16–7.

"In the fourth quarter," Meyer said, "I think we outmanned them."

Outmanned them.

Fulmer finally faced reality. And it was harsh. Out of 117 Division I teams, the Vols ranked 71st or worse in five offensive categories. Tennessee hadn't lost to Florida and still advanced to the SEC title game since 1997. A game at No. 4 LSU was next on the schedule. And Ainge, Fulmer finally admitted, was a mess.

"I think the rotation probably affected Erik to some degree as we've gone along here," Fulmer said.

Finally, Fulmer, his coaches, his players and the media weren't so deceived. And Rick Clausen, the humble, likable, feel-good story of the pre-season, wasn't feeling too good after the Florida game. It turns out that Clausen's comments following the win over UAB were also pretty deceptive.

"The quarterback derby or whatever you want to call it, it doesn't matter," Clausen had said. "Basically, the questions about the whole quarterback thing, I'd like them to stop just because we're worried about winning football games. I'm not worried about who the quarterback is going to be."

Until it wasn't him.

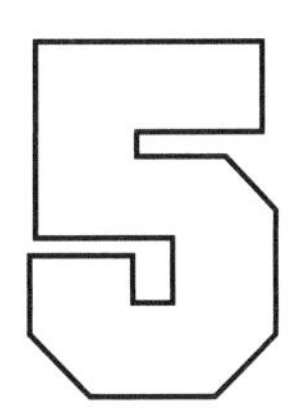

Nobody Knows Anything

One of the most memorable weeks of Rick Clausen's life—and in Tennessee football history—started with Clausen cursing out Phillip Fulmer in his Neyland-Thompson Sports Center office.

Considering the bizarre, often acrimonious events leading up to the Tennessee-LSU game, a string of obscenities from the quarterback's mouth aimed at the head coach was really quite standard.

That same week, University of Tennessee president Dr. John Petersen and athletic director Mike Hamilton exchanged heated barbs with SEC commissioner Mike Slive and LSU athletic director Skip Bertman. Members of the offense fumed at their own production. Parys Haralson's mother, among other parents, exploded at the thought of the Vols playing in Baton Rouge, La., with Hurricane Rita looming in the Gulf of Mexico. And Fulmer exploded because the parents exploded.

Everyone wearing orange was turning red.

Clausen, the popular, laid-back California native, was the first to vent. Clausen was already unhappy before Fulmer called him into his office two days after the loss to Florida. Clausen had supposedly won the job with his performance against UAB but threw just five passes for zero yards in the 16–7 loss to the Gators. He didn't even play in the second half.

Some starting job.

So a grumpy Clausen turned furious when he sat down at Fulmer's desk and found out that Erik Ainge, who was completing 44.2 percent of his passes, was now the starting quarterback. And not just Fulmer's original definition of "starting quarterback." Ainge was the starter—as in, he could throw passes underhanded and not get benched.

"Erik doesn't have to be looking over his shoulder," Fulmer said, and he apparently meant it this time. "It's the same things as before. He gives us a little bit more mobility and a stronger arm. That doesn't mean that he's a lot more mobile or has a lot stronger arm. It just gives us a better opportunity to make plays down the field."

The rotation was over.

"Hindsight is twenty-twenty, and I was trying to be fair to all concerned. Rick had played really well for us. It's not working out," Fulmer said, then hinted that Clausen expressed anger during their meeting. "You know, there's 117 schools in the country, and I'd say there's 117 not-very-happy second-team quarterbacks."

During the week that Clausen expected to face the team that didn't want him, Clausen, in fact, wasn't going to face the team that didn't want him. He was going to sit on the bench at Tiger Stadium, just like he had when he played there. No revenge, no retribution, no payback. The LSU fans would chuckle, and his former teammates would offer a sad smile.

Nothing had changed. Little Clausen was on the bench again.

These were likely the thoughts that circulated through Clausen's head when he cursed at the coach who had rescued him from a potentially dire situation at LSU. And Clausen, who had waited six years for an opportunity to play SEC football, was ready to walk away after coming so close to winning the starting job. Normally the eager quarterback anxious to watch film, Clausen slumped back in his seat during quarterback meetings and paid little attention to Sanders like a bored fifth-grader listening to a monotone history teacher meticulously describe the War of 1812. That Wednesday, Clausen called his parents in California and said he was packing his stuff and coming home.

"It came to the point where I thought I might as well coach Jimmy," Clausen said, referring to his younger brother, also a quarterback. "It came to that point. I just didn't understand. I just didn't understand a lot. It's not my place to understand. He's the head coach, and he makes the decisions. But I really didn't understand at all."

It was the theme of the week. No one understood much inside the Neyland-Thompson Sports Center. "Nobody," as screenwriter William Goldman used to describe Hollywood, "knows anything." And the saying applied to the Vols, particularly on offense.

Terrible. Underachieving. Horrible. Those are just some of the words receiver Jayson Swain used to describe a Tennessee offense ranked 107th nationally in scoring, at twelve points per game, just ahead of Ball State, Temple and Louisiana Monroe. "It's a shame. It's a shame that my middle school team could probably defend this offense right now," Swain said. "That's a shame with all the talent that we have. We need to sit down and figure it out."

Most collegiate teams determine their offensive identity during spring practice or even in recruiting. Some teams develop a power-*I*, shove-it-down-your-throat offense. Some prefer three-wide sets, others go four-wide. Some run to set up the pass; others pass to set up the run. After spring practice, fall camp, two games and a bye week, Fulmer, as he scratched his head with the visor of his white Tennessee hat on a sunny Monday afternoon, admitted Tennessee didn't have an offensive identity aside from going three-and-out.

"I don't think we've established ourselves as to what we want to be yet," he said with almost an embarrassing frown.

Fulmer didn't know if he wanted Tennessee to be run-oriented Navy, pass-happy Texas Tech or somewhere in between. The running game, led by Riggs, wasn't very productive, particularly in short-yardage situations. Riggs' longest run of the season was 16 yards. Clausen wasn't attempting passes downfield, and everyone on the UT sideline covered their eyes when Ainge tried to throw deep. The Volunteers had scored just twenty-four points all season—their lowest total through two games since 1981—and had registered one scoring drive in their last fifteen possessions. All this from a quarterback Fulmer had compared with Peyton Manning at SEC Media Days and a receiving corps touted as one of the nation's best.

"Some say we're supposed to be the best receivers in the nation, some say we've got one of the best quarterbacks in the nation," receiver Robert Meachem said. "That's a lot of talk. If we don't live up to it, why is everybody talking about us?"

Good question. Against man-to-man press coverage during the loss to Florida, Tennessee's receivers rarely got separation and, when they did, Ainge or Clausen failed to get them the ball on several botched deep fades. Swain and Meachem blamed the problems on communication errors between the receivers and the quarterbacks.

"You would think with a year of experience and a year playing with each other that it wouldn't be the case," Swain said. "The Florida game was a case of all the little things that happened making a difference like not seeing the calls. It was just a bunch of little things, and it was terrible. The offense looked horrible. I don't know what's going on."

Even members of the defense, who gave up numerous big plays during Tennessee's first scrimmage, were shocked by the ineptitude of the offense.

"They have an extreme amount of talent on their side of the football," defensive end Jason Hall said. "For whatever reason, they haven't put it together completely yet."

Nobody knows anything.

Including whether Tennessee and LSU were going to play at all in the aftermath of Hurricane Katrina. As Tennessee prepared for Florida, helicopters and ambulances carrying Hurricane Katrina victims frequently landed on the track at LSU, and a medical triage was set up at the Pete Maravich Center, LSU's basketball arena, across the street from Tiger Stadium. LSU's fieldhouse became a special needs unit for evacuees with unique medical issues, and more displaced New Orleans residents stayed at LSU's baseball complex. There wasn't a hotel vacancy within two hundred miles, and the Federal Emergency Management Agency wasn't about to start booting homeless evacuees to make room for an eighteen-year-old waterboy from Tennessee.

In other words, LSU, which had already postponed its season opener against North Texas and would move a home game against Arizona State to Tempe, didn't appear ready to host 90,000 fans, two hundred players, team officials, an SEC officiating crew, a TV production and broadcast team and other media.

Tennessee athletic director Mike Hamilton asked LSU to move the game, scheduled for either 7:00 or 7:45 p.m., to the afternoon so the 7,500 traveling Tennessee fans could find a place to stay on their way home from the game. LSU athletic director Skip Bertman refused, and the SEC didn't intervene.

"We think, at the right time, a football game in Tiger Stadium is going to be a tremendous morale boost in the southeastern areas of Louisiana," said Herb Vincent, LSU's associate athletic director for internal affairs. "So many people follow LSU football around New Orleans. It's going be a rallying event. At LSU, our tradition is to play games at night. We're playing the game at night. It's the right time."

Hamilton bit his tongue and agreed to fly into Baton Rouge, the day of the game—an unheard of practice in major college football—to avoid displacing evacuees from their hotel rooms. Hamilton was in a tricky spot. If he insisted on flying in his team the night before the game, the Vols would be taking away rooms from poor, displaced, homeless, hurricane-weary evacuees. The PR hit would be devastating. Imagine the headlines circulating around a nation starved for hurricane coverage:

"Tennessee Football Team Keeps Evacuees out of Hotel."

And, of course, the subsequent subhead: "'I have no place to stay,' one evacuee said."

No way, Hamilton thought. And Fulmer did his best to put Tennessee's plight in perspective. "With all the hardships those people are going through and have been through, our little bit of an adjustment of the schedule is nothing in comparison," he said.

If Hamilton caused a commotion about LSU insisting on playing the game at night, fans in the Louisiana area would call him insensitive in light of the worst natural disaster to ever hit the United States. We need this game, LSU fans said. We need a return to normalcy, they wrote on Internet message boards. Even when Hamilton suggested ESPN could trade the TV rights to CBS—which televises games at 3:30 p.m.—the LSU message boards erupted with criticism.

We just went through the worst natural disaster in history, and he wants to tell us when we should play the game?

Who does he think he is?

Screw him.

Yeah, screw him.

So Hamilton agreed to play the game at night, tempers subsided, and Bertman, along with the SEC officials, felt good about LSU hosting its first matchup of top-ten teams at Tiger Stadium since 1987.

Until a different hurricane came barreling toward the Louisiana coast.

On the Tuesday before the game, Hamilton contacted the SEC office and told executive associate commissioner Mark Womack the conference should be monitoring Hurricane Rita. Fulmer acknowledged the hurricane was churning in the Gulf of Mexico. "I am concerned about this weather that's apparently coming in, but that's not something that we can do anything about," he said.

On Wednesday, the National Hurricane Center announced Baton Rouge would only get minimal amounts of rain and wind if Hurricane Rita continued on its projected path toward Texas. Hamilton was speaking regularly with Bertman concerning possible weather problems, and the Vols decided to send their managers and trainers, who take a van to road games, to Baton Rouge on Friday morning instead of Thursday.

Thursday was one of the wildest days any reporter on the Tennessee beat could remember. In the morning, cynical reporters who had rolled their eyes about moving the game because of some rain stared blankly at the radar screen. Hurricane Rita, originally projected to slam into the East Texas coast, had taken a slight turn toward Louisiana. Hamilton, Bertman and SEC commissioner Mike Slive met via teleconference early in the afternoon. Hamilton expressed concerns about travel. Bertman said the LSU campus hadn't lost power when Katrina hit, so Baton Rouge should be fine with Rita likely to make landfall in southwestern Louisiana. Slive refused to make a change.

Early that same afternoon, the National Hurricane Center projected heavy winds and rain for Baton Rouge around 11 a.m. on Saturday, the exact time a Delta charter carrying the Tennessee football team was supposed to land at the Baton Rouge Metropolitan Airport. Bumping the game to the end of the season wasn't an option because the SEC championship game wouldn't be moved—which would delay the BCS selections—for one game. It was too late to change venues and play in Knoxville. Hamilton, Bertman, and Slive spoke again. Still no change.

By then, distressed parents of Tennessee football players were besieging Fulmer with phone calls. Most of them wanted to know why the game was still scheduled for Saturday night. Some said they wouldn't let their children on the flight. If the Vols were flying into Baton Rouge on Saturday morning, the mother of Parys Haralson said, Fulmer better find himself a new starter at left defensive end.

The parents weren't the only ones queasy about their children getting on an airplane headed toward a very large hurricane. "I can tell you that about half the guys on our team are not going to fly down there," Ainge said. "They said they would bus or whatever. But they are not going to get on that plane."

Following a day of phone calls from at least twelve worried parents and still no change in the schedule, Fulmer conducted his post-practice interview session at about 5 p.m. in one of the angriest moods—aside from the spring day when police took Robert Ayers and Jerod Mayo out of practice and into jail—anyone on the beat could remember.

"I don't think I'd put my children on a plane. My children aren't going if we go Saturday right now with what I know," Fulmer said. "If the hurricane turns straight south and goes away and ends up in South America, we may look at it differently. I don't see that happening."

Reporters laughed. Fulmer didn't.

"The game should not be played. Not under the circumstances as I understand them," he said. "We bent over backwards to do everything we can to make this game happen, including going down the day of the game. Obviously, if they're sending people out of Louisiana, I don't know why we would be going in. It has to be okay to do in everybody's minds and not just somebody telling us that we're going to be down there."

While Fulmer was trying to express his anger without blasting Slive, UT president Dr. John Petersen was close to doing just that as he joined the teleconference. And to understand why Petersen would be so eager to engage in combat with Slive, you must first understand their history.

In July of 2004, lawyer Tommy Gallion—who was attempting to prove Fulmer was working with the NCAA to bring down the Alabama football program—sent a letter to Slive informing the SEC commissioner that he would serve Fulmer a subpoena at SEC Media Days in Hoover. By handing Fulmer a subpoena in the state of Alabama, Gallion would gain jurisdiction over the Tennessee coach. Fulmer elected to skip SEC Media Days based on the advice of his lawyers and handle interviews by phone.

Slive still fined Tennessee $10,000, infuriating Petersen, who said he mentioned "at least four times" to Slive that Tennessee was averting compliance issues by keeping Fulmer at home. Petersen said Slive understood the argument but refused to budge on the fine during a phone conversation. Some people treat the SEC commissioner, one of the most powerful people in collegiate sports, with reverence. Not Petersen, a well-spoken native of California with a PhD in inorganic chemistry, who didn't follow the formula of smiling and nodding when the commissioner spoke.

"If someone was in a car accident would they have had a $10,000 fine for not being there?" an angry Petersen said. "[Slive] didn't answer me when I asked him that."

Fast forward to September 22, 2005. Slive is still indecisive on moving the game, Bertman still wants to play on Saturday, and now Petersen is on the line. And he's not real happy. "The point I made with the commissioner was, 'You can make whatever decision you think is appropriate. But for us, the final decision will be made depending on what the weather is at that time and whether we feel like it's appropriate to put our people on a plane and send them there,'" Petersen told *The Tennessean*. "That decision was going to overweigh any other decision that was made."

Slive then mentioned the possibility of the Vols forfeiting if they didn't show up for the game. Fine, said Petersen. Hamilton echoed the president's thoughts. "We were ready to do that if that was the case," Hamilton said. "If we felt that it would be unfair to our student-athletes and not safe for our student-athletes, we were prepared to forfeit the game."

At about 6 p.m., Slive relented. No. 10 Tennessee and No. 4 LSU would now play on Monday night at 7:30 p.m.

"After reviewing all of the information I felt this was the best decision for the game," Slive said in a statement. "The safety of our student-athletes, coaches and fans is our priority. I understand this puts a burden on LSU and its administration; however, the travel safety issues necessitate this decision."

Burden on LSU? The statement never mentioned Tennessee was flying in seven hours before the game and losing three preparation days for Ole Miss the following week. Of course, Slive also didn't note the potential compliance issues surrounding Fulmer at SEC Media Days when he announced Tennessee's $10,000 fine in a statement. Hamilton and Petersen bristled.

"They're going to mention what they're going to mention," Hamilton said stoically. "Obviously, Tennessee is inconvenienced as well."

So was Bertman, who argued that a Monday night game

would interfere with campus activities and prevent fans from traveling to the game. LSU associate athletic director Herb Vincent said the school would not refund tickets to Tennessee fans who couldn't make the trip.

"We will now face significant logistical challenges, but we hope for the continued cooperation of our fans," Bertman said. "Naturally, our strong preference would have been to play during the weekend, but safety for student-athletes, fans and everyone else involved in a football game was the overriding factor for the commissioner." So the Vols, after five days of feuds, threats, arguments and cursing, finally relaxed. They wouldn't fly into a hurricane, satisfying players, parents, coaches and fans. Clausen, thanks to a lengthy phone conversation with his parents, chose not to quit the team. And members of the offense, so quick to criticize themselves after looking so wretched against Florida, actually sounded optimistic.

It was as if the hurricane had blown all these problems away.

Ainge was the starting quarterback for good now, and he had the support of his teammates, the same teammates who wondered why Clausen hadn't won the starting job back in fall camp when Ainge was throwing all those interceptions. In an effort to avoid criticizing Fulmer's quarterback rotation, the Vols claimed for weeks they didn't care who was behind center on any given series. After Fulmer admitted he had made a mistake with the quarterbacks and made Ainge the starter, members of the offense finally showed their true feelings.

"We don't have to worry about, 'If Erik messes up this play, then Rick's going to come in, and if Rick messes up this play, then Erik's going to come in,'" tight end Chris Brown said. "I'm glad they finally made a decision. It's great to be settled. I think you'll see everybody rally around more because we know there's one definite quarterback we can rally around and get things done with."

One offensive package. One quarterback. One player to communicate with during the game.

"It will help a lot," center Richie Gandy said. "The thing is, you have two guys in Rick and Erik who are both really good, but who are different styles. Not only does it help us to know who the guy is, but it helps the coaches as far as the game plan. Now the coaches can just go to Erik's strengths instead of putting in more plays for Rick's strengths that Erik might not be so good at."

An offense averaging twelve points per game never felt better. Ainge said he felt like a football player again, his confidence was almost back to Peyton Manning levels, and the silly quarterback rotation, detested by almost everyone on the UT offense, was over. Let's go score some points, the Vols said.

"LSU is going to flip on that tape and see Florida's corners beating up the receivers and us not getting the ball completed down field," Ainge said. "We're a lot better than that. If teams are going to think that's the answer, then I predict we'll have a lot of success."

One question remained: What if Ainge struggled? Like, really, really struggled? What if, say, he threw a no-look underhanded pass out of his own end zone?

"It's still Erik's team, and that's going to be the plan," Fulmer said. "There is no looking over his shoulder. He can go in and just play ball. If he struggles, he's going to get a chance to keep going, pull himself out of it and pull the team out of it."

A quarterback would indeed pull the Vols out of their worst struggles yet.

It wasn't Ainge.

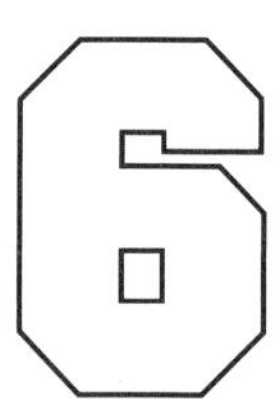

The Comeback

Monday, September 26, in Baton Rouge was a miserably hot day with suffocating humidity and an unforgiving sun. And the people of Louisiana couldn't have been happier. Warm, humid air is a hurricane's energy source, and a heat index of 102 degrees in Baton Rouge with no clouds in the sky meant Rita had released her energy. But, man, it was hot. The following week, right guard Cody Douglas said he'd lost fifteen pounds during the LSU game. It was the kind of day you could work up a sweat simply by drinking a beer.

And that's exactly what LSU fans—who waited three extra weeks for a home football game featuring their beloved national championship hopefuls—did on Monday night. With sticky shirts and an intense passion developed over four weeks of watching chilling tales of destruction in nearby New Orleans, the sight of LSU faithful around Tiger Stadium signaled one of the region's first hints of a return to normal life.

They drank. They partied. They harassed Tennessee.

Two hours before game time, LSU fans rocked four buses carrying the Tennessee party, throwing beer at the windows and screaming obscenities. LSU students, who had all day to drink because the school canceled Monday classes, shook the fourth bus—which carried Hamilton, other school officials and cheerleaders—so violently three windows shattered. Bertman would later issue an apology.

"They were throwing bottles at the buses and that kind of stuff," Hamilton said.

But several sobering reminders of Katrina's destruction were still very evident. Traffic snarled a city hosting thousands of displaced hurricane evacuees. The night before an LSU game is typically a wild affair with music blaring and the smell of Cajun food and barbecue emanating out of RVs. In between bites and drinks, school chants resonate from the hordes of people who gather to celebrate LSU football. On this pre-game Sunday, there were only a handful of people with RVs. They were eating sandwiches.

Ordinarily, about 150,000 LSU fans tailgate before home games, though only 92,400 are fortunate enough to enter Tiger Stadium. On this night, empty seats were noticeable throughout the stadium, including gaping sections in the upper deck. And no orange. Tennessee, with one of the best traveling fan bases in the country, was barely represented because there was nowhere for fans to stay. Hamilton said only five hundred Tennessee fans made the trip, the lowest total in modern school history.

Despite fewer fans on both sides, LSU season ticket holders said a buzz existed inside the stadium like they'd never felt before. The fans needed this game. The region needed this game. The players needed this game. They had spent the last three weeks searching for family members, grimacing at the images on television and watching radar screens. They had housed displaced family members in tiny apartments, walked to class with helicopters flying overhead and, worst of all, gazed at the Pete Maravich Center, LSU's basketball arena, as yet another ambulance dropped off a victim of Hurricane Katrina.

Football hadn't meant much to LSU players over the last month. Same for their fans. As they entered a season with national championship expectations and a new coach, few discussions centered around the quarterback battle between JaMarcus Russell and Matt Flynn. The message boards weren't buzzing with posts about LSU's stout defensive line or the two new cornerbacks or which running back would get the most carries. Fans just wanted to account for their Tiger Stadium friends. The only out routes concerning the players were the ones out of New Orleans and surrounding areas, where family members and friends had lost homes and jobs.

Now, finally, they had a diversion. On this Monday, even for just a few hours, LSU's players and fans could turn away from the grisly scenes in New Orleans and the radars showing the damage and destruction caused by Hurricane Rita to once again experience one of Louisiana's favorite traditions.

A night football game in Tiger Stadium.

A student walked onto the field carrying the New Orleans flag during a pre-game ceremony as the stadium announcer said, "On this evening, we vow to move forward under a common flag because this is LSU football, this is Tiger Stadium, and this is Louisiana." The crowd exploded. The Tigers burst out of the tunnel before coach Les Miles gave them the signal, unable to contain their excitement. The stadium shook. Moments before kickoff, the noise at Tiger Stadium reached such an incredible pitch it seemed the fans fortunate enough to watch the game were trying to make up for the people who couldn't attend. One fan held a sign that read:

> Hurricane Katrina: $30 billion
> Hurricane Rita: $15 billion
> Monday night football at LSU: Priceless!

The Vols, weary from a long flight earlier in the day, had no way of preparing themselves for the emotion LSU players were about to display. They hadn't spent the last four weeks donating clothes, leading blood drives and housing evacuees. Their biggest problem was getting a first down. The Tigers were playing for more than an SEC win. They were playing for a devastated state.

It showed.

On the opening kickoff, LSU's Steve Korte hit Tennessee kick returner Inky Johnson with such ferocity the ball popped loose at the 12-yard line. But officials ruled Johnson down—replays showed it was a close call—and the Vols started deep in their own territory. On Tennessee's first play from scrimmage, LSU's Claude Wroten grabbed Riggs' face mask. On the second play, talented defensive tackle Kyle Williams jumped offsides. The Tigers were playing with so much intensity, so much enthusiasm, they couldn't contain themselves.

On second-and-6, the Tigers put their emotions to good use. LSU's Jessie Daniels blew past UT tackle Albert Toeaina and chased after Ainge, who saw the defensive end coming from the right but, in typical fashion, drifted toward the left and looked downfield for his receivers instead of throwing the ball away or taking a sack. Daniels got there faster than Ainge ever anticipated, knocking the ball loose at the 19 and into the arms of Kenneth Hollis. Fulmer started Ainge over Clausen because of his mobility. On this play, it backfired. Clausen takes the sack. Ainge tries to run.

Nine straight possessions without a point. Clausen began to pace the sideline.

"I wasn't really sure how much I would play or if I would play at all. It was a tough day," he said later. "I had a lot of emotions before the game because I saw a lot of the guys I used to room with and go to school with down at LSU. It was kind of emotional at first."

On LSU's first play from scrimmage, running back Joseph Addai drew Tennessee's linebackers in by running toward the middle of the line. He paused, sprinted to the left into open field and outran Tennessee safety Antwan Stewart to the end zone right in front of the LSU student section. For the first time in more than a month, Louisiana natives had a reason to stand and cheer.

7–0, LSU.

Naming Ainge the starting quarterback was supposed to give the offense more continuity, give the receivers better communication and give Ainge more confidence. Through one quarter, it was giving Fulmer a headache. On the Vols' second drive, Robert Meachem and Bret Smith each dropped passes—at this point, Wide Receiver U was more like, Wide Receiver Who?—and UT took a delay of game penalty. The next possession featured two more Ainge incompletions and a false-start penalty. Tennessee actually managed a first down on the next drive—giving punter Britton Colquitt's foot a much-needed rest—but failed to cross midfield. The Vols punted five times in the first fifteen minutes, fumbled once and extended their scoreless streak to thirteen straight possessions.

"I believe that settling on a quarterback will make a difference for us," Fulmer had said before the game.

Some difference. The Vols were getting worse. And in keeping with the theme of undisciplined play, the Vols bit on a flea-flicker, and Russell completed a 47-yard pass to Craig Davis to set up another touchdown. Forget about the hurricanes. LSU fans were about to trigger an earthquake in Baton Rouge.

14–0, LSU. And Clausen continued to sit as Ainge continued to sputter.

"To be honest, I still kind of thought I'd be on the bench the whole game," Clausen said later.

So did Fulmer, who said he couldn't imagine a scenario, aside from an injury, that would prompt him to bench Ainge. No one could, really. Such a scenario didn't exist until Ainge turned his back on an LSU blitz inside his own end zone. And one of the most remarkable, almost unbelievable tales of redemption truly began.

When the Tigers downed Chris Jackson's second-quarter punt at the 1-yard line, LSU fans rose to their feet in anticipation of Tennessee's last gasp before giving way to the emotion and intensity under the clear Louisiana sky. It was as though they were watching the Vols' offense march from the sideline to the grave, a battered fighter trying to complete one more round. On first down, Ainge couldn't get past the line of scrimmage on a quarterback sneak behind Rob Smith, who sprained his knee on the play but remained in the game. The crowd roared louder.

On the next play, LSU defensive coordinator Bo Pelini thought he could force the shaken Ainge to panic and told his linebackers to blitz against Tennessee's weary line and a hurting Smith. Cameron Vaughn got there first almost untouched, and the description of what Ainge did next depends on whom you ask.

Some say the no-look, almost underhanded pass resembled a hook shot in basketball, which would make sense considering

Ainge's background in the sport. Others suggested Ainge flung the ball like a new bride tossing the wedding bouquet to all her single girlfriends.

Kenneth Hollis caught the bouquet. And he reacted in typical bridesmaid fashion by celebrating wildly after he skipped untouched and unnoticed into the end zone from three yards out. Ainge remained motionless on his stomach after Vaughn's shot knocked him head-first into the goalpost.

21–0, LSU. You could almost hear the TVs in the living rooms across the country switching to the NFL version of Monday night football. Clausen grabbed his helmet.

"I don't think anyone really said anything to me," he would later tell me. "I just saw Erik down. At first, I just thought he was bummed out about the play he just made. But I looked up on the Jumbotron and saw that he hit his head pretty hard on the goalpost, and he kind of stayed down for a little bit. I went and grabbed my helmet. The coaches didn't need to say anything to me. My mindset was perfectly fine by then."

He was the only one. The Vols were now down by twenty-one points on the road. They had gone eighteen straight possessions without scoring a point—A.C. Green never went this long without scoring—Tiger Stadium was starting to shake, the second-string quarterback had almost quit the week before, and the starting quarterback had apparently lost his mind.

"Actually," Randy Sanders would later say, "the goalpost almost went through his mind."

So Clausen trotted onto his former home field to resounding

boos, looked at his stunned teammates in the huddle and, of course, smiled. "Why all the long faces?" he asked.

Members of the offense, who couldn't remember the last time they celebrated a touchdown, couldn't help but relax. Rick, the calm, collected veteran, was back. "When he came in, I felt like it was 0–0," receiver Jayson Swain said. "I think everybody in the huddle felt like it was 0–0, and we had a chance to win. That alone just shows how much confidence we have in Rick."

But not even immediate success by Clausen could rescue the Vols from themselves. The Vols marched down to the LSU 49, where Riggs coughed up the ball following a hit by Ali Highsmith. LSU's Chevis Jackson recovered at the 47. Another turnover. But Clausen didn't lose his composure on the sidelines. He had waited too long for this moment.

"Once we came off the sidelines I told the guys, 'Look how easily we just moved the football,'" Clausen said.

Oddly, the Tennessee locker room was also calm at halftime despite a 21–0 deficit. The fiery John Chavis said he spoke less in the locker room than ever before in his eighteen years at Tennessee. Fulmer never raised his voice or cursed at his players. "I'm not one to throw projectors and hit chalkboards and stuff like that," Fulmer said. "But I've been P.O.ed at halftime before. In this case, the karma just wasn't happening. It was going to happen. It was just like, when is it going to happen? And let's make it happen in this half. I give Rick a lot of credit for that, because he really brought a calmness to the whole team."

This is especially true in the way he runs the offense. Unlike

Ainge, Clausen is fine with dumping off passes to the closest receiver or the fullback if no one is open down field. His first drive of the second half was methodical, time-consuming, a little boring and absolutely perfect against a suddenly conservative LSU defense. It was vintage Clausen. Nine yards to Chris Hannon. Nine more yards to Hannon. Seven yards to Swain. Seven more yards to Swain. Six yards to C.J. Fayton. On second-and-goal, eight yards to Bret Smith for a touchdown.

21–7, LSU.

On Tennessee's first drive of the fourth quarter, it was the same result. LSU's corners played soft, so Clausen unleashed an array of 7- and 8-yard passes in what the media affectionately called the "dink-and-dunk" offense (Clausen despised the term). It was like spanking a child with a wooden spoon. One whack doesn't cause much pain. An accumulation of whacks, however, will cause almost anyone to flinch.

LSU was flinching. Clausen, on fourth-and-goal from the one, snuck into the end zone himself and exploded in anger when one of the LSU players hit him late just across the goal line. Several offensive linemen had to restrain Clausen, and he was still screaming as he jogged to the sideline. Clausen was already motivated to prove himself after Fulmer benched him. He was also driven to erase a twenty-one-point deficit. Now, frankly, he was pissed.

24–14, LSU.

The career of LSU quarterback JaMarcus Russell is remarkably similar to Ainge's time at Tennessee. They both split reps with an older quarterback in an unorganized rotation. They were both noted for their arm strength. Both had even worked at the Manning Passing Academy the previous summer. And they both will amaze you with their talent but ultimately self-destruct with the critical mistake. Ainge had already made his blunder. Now, it was Russell's turn. On third-and-8 from his own 22, Russell forced a pass and was intercepted by Jonathan Hefney, who returned the ball down to LSU's 2-yard line. Two plays later, Riggs rumbled into the end zone with 7:15 remaining.

24–21, LSU.

Tiger Stadium, with just a handful of Tennessee fans in attendance, was eerily silent. And that was before Tennessee got the ball back with 5:24 to play. The Vols blew two chances to take the lead on their first two plays of the drive. Riggs burst up the middle for 22 yards but looked like Nick Harper trying to elude Ben Roethlisberger when he crashed into LSU's LaRon Landry. Riggs had the whole field ahead of him, but couldn't help running into the LSU safety like a magnet hitting a refrigerator. "I had my eye on the end zone," Riggs admitted later. "I probably should have scored a touchdown."

Fine. The Vols still had the ball at the LSU 41 with a new set of downs and plenty of time on the clock. And Sanders still had one of his two surefire touchdown play calls left. Before the game, Sanders said he was almost positive two of his plays would result in touchdowns against certain LSU looks on defense. He called one in the third quarter, and Smith hauled in the 8-yard pass from Clausen for a score. Now, he was overcome with anticipation as he signaled his second and final touchdown play: a pass to fullback Cory Anderson on a wheel route down the left sideline. Anderson would run toward the playside acting as a blocker on play-action, then curve up the sideline as the receivers on his side ran slants to the other end of the field to draw the corners and safeties. Anderson would be wide open. And he executed the route perfectly aside from one minor problem.

He dropped the ball. With no LSU player within 25 yards of him, Anderson dropped a soft pass from Clausen that hit him in stride right in the chest. Fulmer actually fell to the ground with his hands over his face, his headphones and notes scattering everywhere. Sanders stared straight down in disbelief.

"You only have so many touchdown plays going into the game that you really think, 'This has got a chance to be a 40- or 50-yard touchdown,'" Sanders said later. "When you get it called and you get the exact right defense, and you guess exactly right as a play-caller and you get exactly what you want and you don't execute, it's very frustrating."

The Vols settled for a field goal, and LSU settled for overtime when coach Les Miles called a running play for Joseph Addai with 2:02 still left on the clock. The crowd booed loudly. An hour earlier, fans were celebrating in the aisles, briefly forgetting about the hurricanes, no longer worrying about the loss of coach Nick Saban and even leaving the stadium early when LSU took a 24–7 lead in the fourth quarter. Now, they were cursing their new coach in his first home game.

The main source of all their anger was LSU's offensive play-calling. The Tigers abandoned their aggressive style of offense in the second half and gained only 56 yards of total offense in the entire second half. Overtime didn't help settle those nasty sentiments. After Addai gained 11 yards on the first play of overtime, the Tigers handed the ball to sparingly used fullback Jacob Hester—who gained one yard—threw an incomplete pass to Hester and, on third down, Russell threw incomplete again to force a field goal try.

27–24, LSU. The crowd cheered nervously.

The Vols took the field with all of their aspirations, dreams, expectations and goals ready to disappear. Fail to score, and their season would be lost before October. Fail to score, and the critics would point to the off-season mishaps, smirk and say, "Told you so." Fail to score, and they would go down as one of the most underachieving teams of all time. Even some of the Vols acknowledged before the game they were teetering on becoming a punch line.

"It certainly looks silly looking back on it that we were supposed to be, in one poll, I think we were picked to win it all," center Richie Gandy said.

Considering all the praise from coaches, the high marks from voters and the hype surrounding Tennessee in the pre-season, tight end Chris Brown said the glorification "definitely goes to your head."

"I'm sure there was some of that with guys," he said. "You see the pre-season polls and see No. 3 Tennessee, Tennessee this and Tennessee that. Maybe they shouldn't have told us any of that stuff.

Maybe they should have told us we're No. 25 or whatever and let us play. You can't make excuses. That's just the way things are."

Those expectations were long gone by this point. They had faced a twenty-one-point fourth-quarter deficit to the nation's fourth-ranked team and had faced emotional LSU players and fans trying to represent a devastated region. Suddenly underdogs, they had an opportunity on a hot, muggy night in Baton Rouge to redeem themselves and save their season. Fittingly, the two people to handle the ball were Rick Clausen, who had lost his starting job three times in his career—twice at UT, once at LSU—because he wasn't talented enough, and Gerald Riggs Jr., the so-called bust who was wasting his football career. If the Vols were going to shock the critics who had given up on them, the two biggest underdogs on the team would have to do it. All they had to do was get in the end zone. Twenty-five yards separated them from the greatest comeback by an LSU opponent in Tiger Stadium history.

Unlike LSU, the Vols played to win. On the first play, Clausen completed a ten yard pass to Riggs for a first down at the LSU 15. Riggs carried the ball for seven yards before Landry pushed him out of bounds, then picked up five more for a first down at the 3. LSU fans were screaming in terror, the Tigers looked weary, and the Vols were bouncing up and down on the sideline. Another Riggs carry, this time for two yards. Clausen sneaked for no gain, setting up third-and-goal from the 1.

Riggs took the handoff and ran through a hole behind left guard, one occupied by LSU linebacker Cameron Vaughn. Both

Riggs and Vaughn had been highly regarded prospects coming out of high school. Riggs was ranked the nation's No. 2 running back; Vaughn was rated the No. 9 inside linebacker. Both chose to play for their in-state schools. Now, they met face to face with an anxious national television audience and 92,000 fans waiting on the winner. Conquering the bigger Vaughn could define Riggs' career at Tennessee instead of the missed classes, suspensions and unrealized potential. For almost three years, Riggs fought all the negative publicity. But an experience as a teenager had already taught Riggs the true meaning of a battle.

Gerald Riggs Jr. hadn't succeeded in many battles during the first two years of his Tennessee career, falling victim to poor grades, tardiness, injuries, opposing defenses and general immaturity. He kept quiet about his tumultuous first two years in Knoxville, never even confiding in close friend and roommate Cody Douglas, a starter at right guard. He didn't talk about the harsh commentary from Fulmer through the media. Nor about the weekly chewings from then-running backs coach Woody McCorvey. Nor about the academic suspensions or the late arrivals to walk-throughs. Nor even about his lack of playing time.

"He never really expressed anything to me," Douglas said. "Gerald's the type of person who doesn't talk about his problems."

Tennessee fans hold the individual players to the same incredible expectations that they place on the team as a whole. A star in high school should immediately star at Tennessee. Thousands of Tennessee fans congregate on message boards to discuss every recruit's commitment, decommitment or visit to Knoxville. They analyze every statement made by the prospect. These high school stars can't even sneeze without a story appearing on several recruiting websites (and if he did sneeze, why? Is he sick? Was the weather too cold in Knoxville? Does this hurt Tennessee's chances?), and their recruitment is followed obsessively all the way until Signing Day in February. By this time, some fans know these recruits like their own children. And thanks to recruiting rankings, numerous features on websites and local newspapers and Signing Day announcements on national television, the elite high school players are already All-Americans before they ever step on a college campus.

"It's making them celebrities," Fulmer said.

Riggs, who scored sixty-six touchdowns during his final two years at Red Bank High School, was one of these players. So most fans, expecting the highly recruited Riggs to immediately become the next Jamal Lewis at Tennessee, came to this conclusion following his sophomore year: Gerald Riggs Jr. is a bust. He's lazy and immature. What a waste.

"You could go down the list," he said, rolling his eyes.

There was another long list involving Riggs. And it wasn't positive, either. Riggs failed to pass six hours of class during his first fall semester and was suspended for Tennessee's Peach Bowl matchup against Maryland in his hometown of Atlanta. He was also suspended for the first half of the 2003 season opener against

Fresno State for failing to meet Fulmer's academic policies in summer school, and he showed up late for a Friday walk-through later in the season. Rumors surfaced that one of Tennessee's graduate assistants, Shane Beamer, walked Riggs to class every day—all but holding his hand and packing his lunch box—to ensure he showed up instead of sleeping in.

"There's a lot of things I don't agree with that have been said about me," Riggs said. "But if I could just point out one off the top of my head, it would be my maturity and dedication. I've always been dedicated to the game. I think I've matured. There's just certain things growing into a young man I had to learn. I think my situation was a little bit more public than everybody else's situation. But hey, that's the position I put myself in by going out and making plays and being a good player. I welcome that, but at the same time, I think I was unfairly judged in a lot of ways."

Behind the famous name and underneath the straight face, Riggs knew the real meaning of a struggle. A struggle isn't standing on the sideline for an entire game, waiting for a chance to play. A struggle is a twelve-year-old kid trying to comprehend his mom undergoing chemotherapy and losing her hair. Besides, Riggs doesn't need much help from teammates, friends or anyone else. Voicing his concerns isn't going to help. All he needs is Mom. Together, he and Mom can defeat any problem.

Even cancer. Just ask his mother, Druann Riggs.

"My boy, Gerald," said Druann, her voice cracking with emotion, "saved my life."

On July 19, 1996, doctors diagnosed Druann Riggs with breast cancer. She was a single mother raising Gerald in Atlanta, a long way from her family and friends in her hometown of Boston. All she had was Gerald, and he wasn't going to let her down. When Druann began chemotherapy treatment, Riggs shaved his head in a show of unity. Riggs asked his middle school football teammates to do the same, and pretty soon bald-headed twelve-year-olds were blocking for a bald-headed running back who couldn't be tackled. Druann, who refused to miss a game and attended every Tennessee scrimmage in 2005, took delight in her son's sprints to the end zone. Riggs' exploits on the football field, tennis courts and even golf courses consumed her, and it wasn't long until she didn't worry about being sick. He was a menace to his coaches, a recluse to his teammates and a nuisance to the fans at Tennessee, but Riggs was a savior to his mother.

"He gave me all the strength and desire to fight and to make it," Druann said, needing another moment to compose herself, "and I think Gerald learned how to fight and how to make it, and I learned how to fight and make it. We just fed off each other."

And they overcame their problems together. Druann Riggs survived breast cancer. And her son survived the critics. He entered the 2005 season a Heisman Trophy candidate and the starting running back at Tennessee, considered a serious contender for the national championship. The road to winning a national championship and claiming a Heisman Trophy is long. But so is the road just to get an opportunity. Before Riggs could begin his future as a starter, though, he had to revisit his past. One more old, familiar roadblock remained in Riggs' path before he could embark on the promising senior season he had waited his entire career to experience.

Academics. No matter how many conflicting descriptions of Riggs' personality exist, no one close to him can deny one, simple fact about the embattled running back: he doesn't like school. Even Riggs' most staunch defenders, including his own father, were quick to acknowledge academics aren't a priority in the running back's life.

"I think academics is something that he does to play football," running backs coach Trooper Taylor admitted.

And yet, despite all of Riggs' previous academic problems, fans, teammates and members of the media were all surprised when reports surfaced that Riggs needed a stellar summer semester in the classroom to remain eligible for the fall semester his senior year. Tennessee's coaches dodged questions about Riggs' grades for the majority of the summer, simply stating he needed to go to class. But Riggs' father, former NFL star Gerald Riggs, later confirmed his son's academic progress had dipped as a junior and his grades during summer session were vital to his eligibility.

"Gerald lost focus this past year," Riggs Sr. told *The Tennessean*. "He's heard it over and over again that to do it on the field, he has to take care of business in the classroom. He's run that course and been hard-headed about it at times. I think Gerald's grown up considerably in that regard, but kids need parents around them to kick them in the butt. That's still the case with him."

So with the long-awaited chance to be the feature back at

Tennessee, a Heisman Trophy candidate, a member of a national championship-caliber team and a senior looking to impress NFL scouts, Riggs still bordered on becoming academically ineligible. And since the four running backs behind Riggs—Arian Foster, Ja'Kouri Williams, Montario Hardesty and LaMarcus Coker—had a combined zero career college carries, Tennessee's national championship hopes rested on Riggs' summer school report card.

No one really thought Riggs would fail—when had the last star player at UT missed a season due to academics?—but the news shook the confidence of every fan, teammate and coach who believed Riggs had finally begun to mature as a senior. "Believe me, there were times that I didn't think he was going to make it through Tennessee," Riggs Sr. said.

Enter Trooper Taylor, who took the running backs job following the 2003 season when McCorvey joined his friend Sylvester Croom on the staff at Mississippi State as offensive coordinator. One of sixteen children, Taylor is an excitable, talkative Texan who is twenty years younger than McCorvey and acts thirty years younger. While celebrating a touchdown with a player as an assistant coach at New Mexico, Taylor accidentally caught his hand in a player's facemask and suffered a compound fracture of his finger. He broke his ankle running down the sideline at Tulane with a defensive player who was returning a fumble. He once separated his shoulder while delivering a chest-bump and a high-five to one of his players. The playful Taylor was a perfect match for Riggs, who didn't need another coach pointing out his failures. He needed a friend. And Taylor's influence was immediately evident.

Sure, Riggs would rather take a vicious hit from a 250-pound linebacker than go to class. Against Alabama the previous year, he did just that. And to his credit, Riggs learned a lot more about himself on October 23, 2004, than in any biology or history class.

On his second carry against the Crimson Tide, a defender came unblocked off the edge and delivered a punishing shot to Riggs' ribs. He couldn't stand up straight or breathe and headed to the sideline, where he started tasting blood. He felt like he needed to use the bathroom, but he returned to the game and played the rest of the half. At halftime, Riggs finally went to the bathroom and urinated blood. He continued to wipe blood away from his mouth. The trainers said Riggs was bleeding internally, and even Taylor admitted he was scared.

Not Riggs. He carried the ball seventeen more times following the hit in the most meaningful 39-yard performance of his career. "He never flinched, never complained," Taylor said. "He just kept going. That's what you're looking for. That's a warrior. Anybody can talk about it. We say in our room, 'Don't talk about it. Be about it.' Gerald Riggs was about it that day."

Teammates and coaches who knew him only through the criticisms witnessed a side of Riggs on that day only his family knew existed. Riggs had helped his mom beat cancer. A little blood wouldn't slow him down. "Once they found out what really happened, guys were saying, 'Yeah, he is dedicated and he can go out and be as tough as we all heard about and play the game. We can win with this guy,'" Riggs said.

Sure, no one—not even Taylor—could convince Riggs academics were important to his career. But he cruised through summer school academically eligible and headed into the fall as the feature back, a Heisman Trophy candidate and blessed with a new nickname: "Seabiscuit." Since Riggs was a dark-horse candidate for the Heisman Trophy and his slow-starting career was similar to that of the horse, Seabiscuit, whose story had recently been turned into a movie, Taylor and the Tennessee running backs dubbed Riggs with the moniker. "He's a broke-up guy trying to come back and win, like Seabiscuit," Taylor said. "He said that makes me the blind jockey. I'm going to work on my weight, and he's going to work on his wind."

Riggs was running with a purpose on this steamy night in Baton Rouge. A game-winning touchdown run would reinforce his rising status among the nation's backs and give him a better chance of taking care of his mother.

Just like she was taking care of him.

"She's worked hard her whole life to keep me afloat and to help me get through the tough times," Riggs said. "She's been there through a lot. It'd mean a lot to me to do something for her and to make her happy. Hopefully, if things go right and I stay healthy and play some good football, I can make the kind of money to take care of her because she's done a lot, and she really deserves it."

Druann Riggs tried but couldn't hold back tears when told of her son's words. I don't deserve it, she said. He does.

He saved her life.

Now, Seabiscuit was about to ride. Riggs was running to prove he belonged among the top Tennessee backs. He was running to give fans a reason to remember him other than his mistakes, to meet the expectations he'd placed upon himself, to give his mom another reason to smile and to save Tennessee's season. Like Vaughn was going to stop him. Pumping his legs furiously, Riggs overpowered Vaughn at the goal line and scored the game-winning touchdown standing up. He simply wanted it more. Riggs dropped the ball, then looked up at the sky. It was as though he were watching all of his troubles disappear into the night air as his teammates in orange swarmed him.

Except for one. Clausen picked up the ball and made one of the most memorable passes of his life, unleashing six years of frustration and constant disappointment by heaving the ball into the LSU student section.

30–27, Tennessee.

The following day, Clausen said, "I just wanted to say, thanks for all the good times, thanks for harping on me and writing articles like you did while I was there saying I wasn't good enough to play there. I just wanted to say that I can play."

Hollywood would laugh at this script and call it unbelievable. An undersized kid considered the least talented of his brothers signs with LSU, only gets one start before the coach tells him to start looking elsewhere if he wants to play, is released without much fanfare to Tennessee, where he serves as a third-team quarterback. The following year, one week before playing his former team, he's benched again, throwing only five passes in the previous game. He almost quits the team, then comes back to lead Tennessee to 30 points after halftime in the biggest comeback ever witnessed at Tiger Stadium, the place he used to call home.

It was hard to tell if Clausen even enjoyed the moment immediately following the game. Fulmer heaped praise on him during a post-game ESPN interview only to realize his quarterback was staring straight ahead. On national television, following the defining moment of his career, Clausen refused to acknowledge his coach. The tension was felt across the entire nation.

"I don't know if there has ever been a better story than Rick Clausen," Fulmer said, getting no reaction from his quarterback. "I really don't, in all of college football. He's a tough-minded guy. He obviously had to handle the disappointment at the beginning of the week, and he handled it with toughness and class. His teammates rallied around him. Getting done what he got done was unbelievable.

"He was mad as heck with me and should have been. I admire him, and I love him. He probably doesn't love me a whole lot right now, but I do."

Clausen silently stuck it to his coach on national television, then headed to the locker room to do an ESPN Radio interview. After changing clothes, Clausen walked back onto the field, stopped at the 30-yard line and gazed at empty Tiger Stadium. He thought of his first college experience, the fans who used to cheer for him and what he'd just accomplished against old roommates, coaches and friends. Clausen later called the moment "surreal." He had asked a team manager to retrieve his cell phone from the locker room. Clausen took the phone and called home, where his parents watched the game on television because they couldn't get a flight into Baton Rouge. When he'd spoken with his parents the previous week, they had talked him out of quitting the team. Just a few days later, he was a hero. In the span of twelve hours, the Vols had flown to Baton Rouge, fallen behind by twenty-one points, saved their season and found their new quarterback.

"It kind of hit me a little bit once I was talking to my mom because I walked out onto the field, and it was kind of quiet," Clausen said. "That's when it really hit me."

Only then did Clausen realize he had led the biggest comeback in Tiger Stadium history against the nation's fourth-ranked team. Only then did Clausen realize he had led an offense with twenty-four points all season to thirty points after halftime against one of the SEC's most feared defenses. Only then did Clausen realize he had proved coaches and players on both sidelines wrong in about two hours. Yes, this was the ultimate redemption.

"I think it tested me more than any other life lesson that I've had," Clausen said. "It was a very tough week. Besides a tragedy in the family or a tragedy around it, it was probably one of the toughest weeks I've ever had to deal with just because of the fact that something that I've worked for about five or six years almost didn't happen."

Clausen had also waited five or six years to become a full-time starter, which happened the following day.

It would seem like five or six years before it was all over.

7

Disaster Strikes:

How UT Loses Four in a Row

IF YOU'RE TRYING to determine who will be the most dominant football team in the SEC, start by finding out where Rodney Garner is working.

Research all the statistics, coaching records, number of returning starters and strength of schedule all you want in search of the perfect formula for a successful SEC team. The most accurate trend is much simpler: where Garner, a personable, hard-working, extraordinary recruiter from Leeds, Ala., works, championships usually follow. Following an abbreviated stint in the Arena Football League in 1989, Garner started his coaching career at Auburn—where he played defensive tackle for four seasons—as the assistant strength and conditioning coach. He was quickly elevated to recruiting coordinator, and in 1993, Auburn rebounded from two straight five-win seasons to finish 11–0. Probation prevented the Tigers from playing for a national championship, but they were widely considered the best team in the nation. (Florida State, with a 12–1 record, won the national title.)

Following the 1995 season, Auburn coach Terry Bowden settled a rift in the coaching staff by firing two assistants, including Garner. Recruiting-minded Tennessee coach Phillip Fulmer immediately offered Garner a full-time job as an assistant coach in 1996, and the results were almost immediate. The Volunteers won the SEC championship in 1997, their first national title in forty-seven years in 1998 and fielded one of the most talented teams in school history in 1999 (but went 9–3). Citing the need to be closer to his wife's family in Augusta, Ga. and Jacksonville, Fla., Garner bolted for Georgia after the 1997 season to serve as recruiting coordinator and defensive line coach under Jim Donnan.

"Fans didn't understand, but I definitely think Coach Fulmer understood," Garner said at the time. "If I had to do it over again, I would do it again."

Bowden, now out of coaching, reportedly said Garner was "trouble," and he would land Georgia some NCAA violations, not championships. It was a common perception with Garner, who bristles at any accusations of cheating and accurately points out he's never been in any trouble with the NCAA. But he was too good to be true, and those are NFL defensive tackle Albert Haynesworth's words.

Haynesworth said Garner's in-home visits, which included taking the high school star to the Columbia, S.C. mall, were perfect. Haynesworth also said his recruiting visit to Georgia in 2000 was perfect. Too perfect.

"I thought, 'Man, you can't go here. You know it can't be like that all the time,'" Haynesworth told the *Athens Banner-Herald*, and he didn't go there. He signed with Tennessee.

But most highly rated recruits were enamored with Garner. Georgia head coach Mark Richt retained Garner in December of 2000, and, two years later, the Bulldogs won their first SEC championship in twenty years. In Richt's first four years at Georgia, Garner helped the Bulldogs win forty-two games, an SEC title, two SEC East championships, three bowl games and finish in the top six nationally three times. Richt, deservedly, received the acclaim and the enormous raise. But if Garner—not Richt—left Athens, most recruits admitted they wouldn't even consider traveling down Georgia's Highway 316 East to the Classic City.

"To be honest, we felt that way too," said Don Shockley, the father of Georgia quarterback D.J. Shockley. "Everybody in the recruiting business has got their little song and dance, but you ask yourself, can you trust them with your child? And around here, everyone trusts Rodney."

Fans and college football programs appreciate him even more when he's gone. Auburn wasn't the same for almost a decade after Garner left. And Tennessee hasn't yet recovered. Fulmer used to agitate Bulldog fans by plucking the best talent out of Georgia every winter, including all-conference stars Jamal Lewis, Deon

Grant and Cosey Coleman. In 2002, Fulmer didn't sign a single player out of Georgia. In 2003, he signed two—Bill Grimes (now a reserve receiver with zero career catches) and defensive back Jarod Parrish, who plays sparingly. Georgia didn't recruit either player. In 2004, Fulmer landed only two more Georgia prospects—unheralded defensive back Inky Johnson and offensive lineman Cameron Mayo, who is the son of former UT star Bill Mayo. Not exactly Jamal Lewis and Deon Grant.

The result? After beating Georgia nine straight times from 1989–99, the Vols had lost four out of five to the Bulldogs entering their game October 8 at Neyland Stadium. Tennessee, as an SEC bad boy along with Florida, used to irritate Georgia fans more than any other school. Sure, the Bulldogs seemingly never beat Florida, but those games were 370 miles away at a neutral site in Jacksonville, Fla. Every two years, the Vols would strut into Sanford Stadium, annoy the red and black faithful with the constant sounds of "Rocky Top" and blast Georgia. Before the 1998 game, confident Georgia students excitedly discussed storming the field when they finally beat Tennessee. The Vols won, 22–3.

But the Bulldogs no longer feared Tennessee. They even administered a 41–14 beating of the Vols at Neyland Stadium in 2003—very nearly UT's worst home loss since 1904—and were now going for three straight wins in what used to be the most daunting place to play in the SEC. Now, it seemed opponents were lining up along the Tennessee River to play inside Neyland Stadium.

Neyland Stadium is the third-largest college football venue in the country, considered one of the top settings for a game by several publications and had been half-empty by halftime in Tennessee's last four meetings against top-ten teams. Here's a stat not found among the glowing reviews of Neyland Stadium: since defeating No. 10 Georgia in 1999, the Volunteers were 0–5 against top-ten teams at home, including four straight losses by an average of almost twenty-three points. In each of those four meetings, thousands of empty beige seats at Neyland Stadium were noticeable as the bands performed their halftime show.

This year, thought the Tennessee faithful, would be different. Despite Garner's efforts, the Vols were certainly more talented than Georgia in 2005. As a less talented team the previous season, Tennessee actually went to Athens and stunned the third-ranked Bulldogs, 19–14. Now, the Vols were brimming with confidence after shocking LSU in one of the most unlikely wins in school history and then defeating Ole Miss 27–10 at home five days later, which Fulmer counted as revenge against the Rebels firing of his good friend and former assistant David Cutcliffe. New Ole Miss coach Ed Orgeron also irked Fulmer by saying he was "going to build a fence around Memphis" in reference to recruiting. "I guess there's no fence around Memphis," Fulmer said wryly after the game.

Mercifully, the Vols had also finally found their quarterback in Clausen. For real this time. Erik Ainge never left the sideline against Ole Miss, his last pass still the bridal bouquet toss at LSU. "I hope all this quarterback talk is over, and Rick's our guy, and we're going to move on and play the rest of the season that way," receiver C.J. Fayton said.

Clausen was even getting along with his coach again after Fulmer publicly and privately apologized for benching him without much of a reason. "It shows he's a man," Clausen said. "I think that's the biggest thing. If you do something wrong, you usually say you did something wrong. He did that. It's basically water under the bridge now."

But these were the 2005 Vols, so good feelings never lasted long.

Freshman running back Montario Hardesty, a highly rated prospect with huge, strong thighs, who had surprised teammates in summer workouts by consistently outrunning all of them up a steep incline, tore his ACL against Ole Miss and was lost for the season just as he was starting to solidify himself as Gerald Riggs Jr.'s top backup.

One week after leading one of the great comebacks in school history, beating his former team and proving his own coach wrong on national television, the normally agreeable Clausen was irritated once again. First, he had been pissed at the head coach. Now, he was ticked at the fans who grumbled during the Ole Miss game. Clausen appeared to miss several open receivers down field, causing the fans to murmur in the stands, and his longest completion was a 25-yard screen pass to Arian Foster. Clausen completed only eighteen of thirty-five passes and didn't throw a touchdown.

The honeymoon was already over. In a more loquacious mood

than usual, Clausen addressed the media on Monday after the Ole Miss game and didn't just want to talk about his two dislocated fingers, bruised throwing shoulder, and an aching Achilles' tendon that would require him to wear a protective walking boot for most of the week.

"I think there were a few guys open that I just didn't see, but that's not in my progression," Clausen said. "I heard the fans rumble a little bit, but they don't understand what our progressions are. They don't understand our reads and checks we have to make. If guys are running open down the field and I don't see them, then either I didn't see the guy or it's not my progression. A lot of people say I've got that dink-and-dunk kind of offense or whatever. But ever since I've stepped on the field, we've put points on the board. Last year, we did the same thing. This year, we're putting points on the board again. Maybe not as many as we hoped to start the year off. But we're moving the football, and the points will come."

Clausen was rolling now.

"We had four days of practice for Ole Miss. We played a Monday night game, and then we had four days of practice for Ole Miss. A lot of people are critical about the Ole Miss game, but hey, we had four days to prepare for them. So, people can be critical all they want. Sometimes guys just weren't open. Sometimes guys weren't where I thought they would be. Rather than take a sack or force something and make a mistake, I throw the ball away. That might go down as an incompletion and people booing or doing what they do, but that's fine. I can take that."

What Clausen refused to clarify was his statement that wide-open receivers weren't in his progression. That's because, in typical Clausen fashion, he was protecting his teammates. Clausen didn't see those open receivers because they were running the wrong routes. He just didn't want to use the media to call them out, so he took the blame.

No wonder his teammates loved him. And at the other end of the spectrum was linebacker Daniel Brooks. Rated one of the best linebackers in the country coming out of Central-Merry High School in Jackson, Tenn., back in 2003, Brooks drew comparisons to former UT star Al Wilson—who played at the same high school—because of his ferocious play and tremendous speed. But Brooks saved the biggest hits of his Tennessee career for frat boys. He was linked to three fights at fraternity parties in the span of just more than a year and once chased a frat member through the Kappa Sigma house with such venom the poor kid elected to jump off the balcony—breaking his foot—instead of facing the angry Brooks.

Brooks had far less success hitting padded men carrying a football, recording eleven tackles in two seasons and earning a three-game suspension for the 2005 season. Al Wilson was a running back's nightmare and a leader who commanded more respect than perhaps anyone who ever wore the orange and white. Daniel Brooks, as it turned out, was quite the opposite of Al Wilson.

Brooks had been involved in a fight just days before the 2004 SEC championship game. Now, five days before one of the biggest games of the year, Brooks got into an on-campus scuffle with basketball players Andre Patterson and Jemere Hendrix. The trio apparently exchanged words at a private party following the Ole Miss game over a female guest. Brooks wasn't supposed to be there as part of his punishment from Fulmer. Brooks told Fulmer the two basketball players confronted him on campus the next Monday, and Hendrix threw a punch before Tennessee defensive end Jason Hall helped break up the fight. Fulmer had heard enough, finally kicking Brooks off the team for violating curfew. In the ultimate irony, Brooks, who somehow never faced legal trouble for his brawling, threatened to sue Hendrix for attacking him. Tennessee basketball coach Bruce Pearl also dismissed Hendrix. "We have made every effort to help Daniel work through some issues," Fulmer said.

So one week after beating two conference teams and reasserting themselves in the SEC championship race, the eighth-ranked Vols lost a promising running back to a season-ending injury, a linebacker brawled with members of the basketball team and was dismissed, the quarterback was hurting and starting to get annoyed with the fans and the offense was back on life support.

Welcome to the 2005 season.

It would only get worse. Much worse.

The Georgia Game:

"If the fans bail on us now, they're not true fans."

The Georgia game provided the fans and media the first serious inclination that some of Tennessee's problems had more to do with coaching than everyone first believed. First, there was the strategy. Tennessee featured one of the most feared defenses, particularly against the run, in the entire country. The week before, Ole Miss barely escaped rushing for negative yards and considered getting back to the line of scrimmage on an off-tackle run a minor victory. Meanwhile, Tennessee's offense sputtered more than a 1984 Yugo climbing the Smoky Mountains and made more mistakes than Elizabeth Taylor in a wedding dress. Conventional wisdom states that coaches should take advantage of rare scoring opportunities knowing the defense will clean up any field position mess.

"Put it on our backs," linebacker Kevin Simon had said. "I'd rather have it on the backs of our defense than the offense."

But facing elimination from the SEC East title chase against the nation's No. 5 team, Fulmer was playing not to lose rather than playing to win. In the first quarter, the Vols faced second-and-1 at the Georgia 37. Riggs lost a yard, Clausen threw an incomplete pass and Fulmer, playing a field position game, elected to punt from the 38. Britton Colquitt's kick went just 22 yards, and Georgia took over at the 16.

By the fourth quarter, Tennessee was trailing by thirteen points with 6:36 remaining, and Fulmer's decision to punt from the UT 35 surprised the Bulldogs so much they called a timeout. Fans erupted in boos, then headed toward the exits—at this point, they're known as escape routes when a ranked team comes to Neyland Stadium—to avoid watching the inevitable conclusion. Smart move. Georgia marched down the field and scored to take a 27–7 lead.

But more indicting than Fulmer's strategy was the obvious indication that his message in the meeting rooms and on the practice field was not getting across to the players, who would later say the coaching staff overlooked most of the mistakes made during practice. These included simple fundamentals. The Vols were a talented, veteran bunch, the staff figured. They wouldn't make those mistakes in the game.

Only they did. Lots of them. The Vols committed twelve penalties for 78 yards, turned the ball over three times and looked completely inept on special teams. Clausen threw high to a wide-open Bret Smith in the end zone before throwing an interception. On Georgia's first scoring drive, which culminated in a Brannan Southerland 1-yard touchdown run, the Vols jumped offsides twice. On the Vols' next possession, right tackle Albert Toeaina lined up wrong, allowing Charles Johnson to charge untouched toward Clausen and cause a fumble, which led to a field goal and a 10–0 halftime lead. On Tennessee's first drive of the third quarter, talented offensive tackle Arron Sears jumped offsides on two straight plays, and an illegal block by Rob Smith erased an 11-yard run by Riggs. The Vols punted. (Fulmer would later vehemently protest the chop block call on Smith, but Jonathan Wade intercepted Shockley on the first play following the punt, and Clausen scored one play later to cut Georgia's lead to 13–7. The chop block call was a blessing in disguise for the Vols.)

On third-and-6 from the UT 5 in the fourth quarter, Clausen inexplicably threw a three-yard pass to Jayson Swain, and the Vols were forced to punt yet again. Colquitt, instructed earlier in the week not to punt the ball down the middle of the field to dangerous UGA returner Thomas Flowers, promptly punted the ball down the middle of the field to Flowers, who returned it 54 yards for a touchdown to give Georgia a 20–7 lead. Tennessee's special teams were anything but special. The Vols started drives from their own 6-, 7- and 8-yard lines thanks to two penalties on kickoff returns and another on a punt return.

"The penalties in the kicking game are silly and stupid things that are going on," Fulmer said. "Guys aren't listening well enough."

And on a day when Tennessee honored the 1985 "Sugar Vols," a team recognized for accomplishing so much with so little, the 2005 Vols continued to accomplish so little with so much. National championship hopes were finished. It took all of five games for Tennessee's aspirations of winning national and SEC titles to evaporate, culminating in a 27–14 loss to Georgia on a cloudy, dreary Saturday. As Georgia players walked off the field pumping their helmets toward the cluster of fans wearing red and black, several Vols and defensive line coach Dan Brooks stood at midfield, the players still wearing their helmets, to protect the *T*. In 2001, the Bulldogs had jumped on the *T* in celebration after beating Tennessee. This time, several Georgia players walked past the *T*, surveyed the scene and laughed at the Vols.

"Too late," Georgia running back Tyson Browning said. "We already took it."

Tennessee players protected their beloved *T*, but they still weren't protecting Neyland Stadium. The Vols had lost their sixth straight game at home to a top-ten team, the last five by thirteen points or more.

"We need to play better against the good people," Fulmer said, one of the few correct judgments he made all day. The Vols were now 3–2 and appeared lost on offense and special teams. Only Wade's interception and a meaningless touchdown as time expired prevented a shutout on their own field. And then you start remembering all those awful practices Fulmer had bemoaned during fall camp. And then you remember all the issues with discipline. And then you remember all those foreboding lightning strikes and David Ligon's injury on the first play of the first scrimmage.

And then you start to think the Vols were doomed in 2005.

Cornerback and leading tackler Jason Allen, a potential second-round pick in the NFL draft the previous season who wanted to play his senior year, suffered a gruesome hip injury during the second quarter when massive Georgia tight end Leonard Pope trampled him following a catch. Allen was lost for the season. And during the post-game press conference, Clausen erupted for the third time in less than three weeks.

"We're playing for everybody in the Tennessee family," he boldly stated. "I'm sure some of the people out there are going to pack us in and say, 'It's not worth it.' If that's the way they feel, that's fine. We're going to keep playing. We've got enough pride in ourselves. If the fans bail on us now, then apparently they're not true Tennessee football fans."

Funny Clausen should disown Tennessee fans who were down

on the program, since Clausen himself had threatened to quit the team just two weeks before. But that had been before Clausen became a hero, before Fulmer was back in good graces with the fans, and the Vols were in the top ten again ready to compete for a spot in the SEC title game. It had been only twelve days ago. It seemed like twelve weeks. Near the stadium after the game, a group of Tennessee fans with cameras poised stood around an orange port-a-potty and chuckled.

Someone had spray-painted "Fulmer's house" on the port-a-potty door.

The Alabama Game:
"Phillip Fulmer is a (expletive) (expletive)."

Five police officers surrounded and shielded a visitor who stepped off the bus onto the pavement of Bryant Drive and walked toward Bryant-Denny Stadium. Two more police officers would escort the visitor's family, even if they were simply making a pre-game trek through a press box full of hungry sports writers. Alabama native Condoleezza Rice, the United States Secretary of State, was in town for the ceremonial coin toss before the much-anticipated Tennessee-Alabama game on October 22.

The security, however, belonged to Phillip Fulmer, head football coach of the Tennessee Volunteers, and his wife and daughters.

The ride down Tenth Avenue on a gray Saturday afternoon in Tuscaloosa, Ala., was unusually entertaining, quite educational for some younger fans and somewhat disturbing. The crimson-clad fans hanging out on apartment and fraternity house balconies were waving beers and banners, and from the look of the signs dangling from those balconies, you might have imagined a parade was coming through town to honor the death of a tyrant, not the arrival of a college football coach.

"Fat Phil loves to squeal!" one sign read. Others weren't so considerate.

Alabama fans have despised Fulmer passionately ever since local lawyer Tommy Gallion released documents stating Fulmer secretly tape-recorded a conversation with Tide recruiting analyst Tom Culpepper concerning alleged recruiting violations by former assistants Ivy Williams and Ronnie Cottrell at Alabama. Fulmer turned over the information to the NCAA in 2000, Williams and Cottrell, represented by Gallion, went to court, Alabama went on probation in 2001—two of the major violations included a booster giving former prospect Kenny Smith $20,000 and Tide booster Logan Young paying $150,000 to lure Memphis' Albert Means to Alabama—and Tide fans grumbled about Fulmer. Now, the documents proved Fulmer had participated in the fact-finding, and Gallion, ever the conspiracy theorist, claimed Fulmer and the NCAA were working together to bring down the Alabama football program. Alabama fans exploded. While on probation, the Tide went 4–9 in 2003 and 6–6 in 2004, and Fulmer was to blame.

Then the documents, which featured Fulmer's home phone number, cell phone number and home address hit the Internet even though the NCAA had promised him anonymity. Fulmer acknowledged in July of 2005 that Alabama fans had called his cell phone with death threats. But Wally Renfro, the spokesman for NCAA president, Myles Brand, said the NCAA hadn't presented any of the information Fulmer provided to the Committee on Infractions. And Fulmer wasn't the only coach to rat on Alabama. Arkansas coach Houston Nutt said he had been subpoenaed to appear before a grand jury in Memphis to share his experiences recruiting against Alabama in the state of Tennessee. While coaching at Florida, Steve Spurrier wrote a letter to then-Alabama coach Mike Dubose in 2000 threatening to tell the NCAA about alleged recruiting violations. And former Auburn coach Terry Bowden told the NCAA a booster paid defensive lineman Kenny Smith, from Stevenson, Ala., to sign with the Tide.

"We had information from a number of sources, quite frankly a number of coaches, all of whom were concerned about what they saw as a real recruiting issue around activities in the state of Tennessee," Renfro told *The Tennessean.*

Didn't matter to Alabama fans, who aimed all their venom at the overweight—fans also chanted "Krispy Kreme" at Fulmer—old, hated coach who had beaten their team seven straight times from 1995 to 2001, then again in 2003 and 2004. Now he was in Tuscaloosa. The heart of enemy territory. Auburn used to be the most hated team in this part of Alabama. Almost bashfully, several Alabama fans admitted they now hated Tennessee more than Auburn.

"Phillip Fulmer is a lying (expletive)," a fan said with a straight, almost menacing look on his face as he stood outside the stadium. "(Expletive) him. Phillip Fulmer is a (expletive) (expletive)."

Not (expletive) Ivy Williams. Not (expletive) Ronnie Cottrell. Not (expletive) Mike DuBose. Not (expletive) Steve Spurrier.

(Expletive) Fulmer.

"He's a wanted man here," a more rational fan, Tuscaloosa's Scott Wilson, explained before the game.

Fulmer downplayed the fiasco awaiting him in Tuscaloosa, leaving Alabama beat writers who dialed into his weekly Sunday teleconference disappointed. He had addressed the situation at SEC Media Days in Birmingham, he said. He wasn't discussing it again. "It's always a big ball game whenever you play Alabama, and I'm sure there are feelings there," Fulmer said. "That doesn't have anything to do with what happens on the field."

Any other year, reporters would roll their eyes at Fulmer's political answer. But this season, Fulmer did indeed have bigger problems than a drunken Alabama fan screaming the names of donut shops from a balcony. Five games into the season, the quarterback situation was still unresolved—Randy Sanders told the Knoxville Quarterback Club that Erik Ainge would probably play against the Tide—the Vols, national championship contenders two months ago, were virtually eliminated from winning the SEC East, and the offense still had no identity.

Against Georgia, the Vols ran the ball out of the spread offense and gained just 48 yards on the ground. Talented fullback Cory Anderson, who normally averages fifty plays per game but got just twenty-three snaps against Georgia, wasn't real happy.

"It's real disappointing," Anderson said. "I wanted to help the team more than I did, and I didn't get the chance to."

Riggs, who rushed for 1,107 yards the previous year and who was now the feature back on a team ranked 100th nationally in rushing offense, wasn't real happy.

"Ever since I've been playing running back, I've been playing in the 'I' system and have been pretty successful at it," Riggs said. "I try to be careful when I say this, but I think we could always take on new ideas. It's like anywhere else, kind of like a place like Nebraska. They ran the option for so long, and it pretty much became that's the way it was going to be and came back to bite them a little bit in the last couple of years before they changed up."

The offensive linemen, who prided themselves on punishing opposing defensive linemen but were now run-blocking from a stance instead of putting a hand on the ground, weren't real happy.

"It's puzzling to me," said left tackle Arron Sears.

And Fulmer, who said he was "embarrassed" the Vols ranked 96th nationally in scoring offense and 91st in passing efficiency, spent an excessive amount of time with his offensive staff Monday after the Georgia game and was in a very foul mood during the off week before playing Alabama. Fulmer isn't one to cuss like a sailor. He uses profanity about like most football coaches in their mid-fifties. In front of writers, however, Fulmer has the ability to immediately substitute "heckuva" and "darn" into conversation without flinching. And in front of TV cameras, Fulmer clams up like a mobster on trial. Nothing—*nothing*—infuriates Fulmer more than receiving an unexpected, loaded question while TV cameras are rolling. Ask those questions off to the side, he has often said.

All of which makes his response to yet another question concerning the quarterback situation more shocking. Fulmer complained about someone asking who was going to start at quarterback, then actually exclaimed, "Shit!" in his own Tennessee twang to complete the answer in front of TV cameras. The scene was replayed on the local news with the expletive bleeped out. Fulmer was also getting defensive.

"Last year, we won five or six games by six points or less because we took care of the football, because we didn't drop passes, because we made plays. This year, it hasn't exactly happened the same. And we've played a very tough schedule, too," Fulmer said. "What do you do? You come back to the practice field, and you work on it. This staff and this football team, this staff particularly, has won a lot of football games here. I believe we know what we're doing. You address problems and try to get problems corrected as fast as you possibly can. We've had an unusual number of things that have happened to us. We had sixty-three plays against Georgia and fifty-four of them were outstanding plays, well-executed plays. We had twelve mistakes by different people that ended up costing you down and distance, field position or points. That's too many."

Nice math, Archimedes. Not only had Fulmer make the obvious math mistake of 63 – 54 = 12, but no one was sure how he had come up with twelve mistakes, or nine, or whatever he meant.

Reporters came up with almost twenty poor offensive plays after watching tape of the game. Linebacker Kevin Simon did his own math during a seniors-only meeting to discuss the future of the season the Monday before playing Alabama and came up with a conclusion of his own. Simon didn't guarantee a win Saturday against Alabama. He just said the Vols wouldn't lose.

"We're not going to lose this football game," Simon said. "We're not going to be 3–3. No one came from Hawaii or Florida or Texas or up north in New Jersey, no one came here to be 3–3. We're not a .500 ball club. So pretty much from here on out, we're not losing any more football games. We've got our minds made up. It's really not guaranteeing a victory. It's about having a will to win and a desire to get back on top and play our ball game. Every field we've stepped onto this year, we've been the most talented team. We haven't put *W*s up. But I think we've got our swagger back."

So with a new swagger, a new offensive identity—Fulmer now decided he was going to play power football again—and a new quarterback, Ainge, back in the mix, the Vols went down to Tuscaloosa and turned in the same old offensive performance.

In a battle of two stout defenses and two questionable offenses, most college football analysts expected a low-scoring game. Just not a game with, you know, no scoring at all. Both offenses looked as though they were running in mud and carrying footballs covered in oil. The only way to survive watching a replay of the first half would have been to turn down the volume, crank up some circus music and play the tape in fast-forward.

First quarter: Costly false-start penalty on Tennessee forces a punt; Alabama's Keith Brown fumbles after a 7-yard catch; Riggs fumbles at the Alabama 8-yard line after he's already picked up a first down; Alabama misses a field goal; and an illegal formation on the Vols erases a 10-yard run by Riggs. They punt again.

Second quarter: Alabama turns the ball over on downs; Tennessee loses ten yards on a reverse and punts; Alabama quarterback Brodie Croyle takes a sack on third-and-8; Tennessee turns the ball over on downs; Croyle takes *another* sack on third-and-8; and the Vols run out the clock to end the half.

Halftime score: 0–0. We knew the Secretary of State was here, but the Secretary of Defense would have been proud. The loser of this game, it appeared, was going to be the team that made the most critical errors, and, of course, Tennessee was more than happy to oblige.

With 3:19 left in the third quarter and still no score, Tennessee freshman Lucas Taylor, who was getting a chance to return kicks following Jonathan Hefney's fumbled punt against Florida, fumbled a punt of his own at midfield, and Alabama star DeMeco Ryans recovered. Then the Vols committed a 15-yard personal foul penalty to give Alabama one of just two first downs on the drive.

Mistake, mistake. Jamie Christensen booted a 33-yard field goal as time expired in the third quarter, giving the Tide a 3–0 lead. A 41-yard kickoff return by Taylor, who was trying to redeem himself following the muffed punt, and a 35-yard pass from Clausen to Jayson Swain set up a 33-yard field goal by James Wilhoit with 11:46 remaining. After all the mistakes and ineptitude on offense, the Vols were tied with undefeated Alabama on the road in the fourth quarter. But, again, these were the 2005 Vols, so even the seemingly great moments came with an asterisk. Here's the best description of UT's offense, via a message board entry following the Alabama game: "Defending Tennessee's offense is like encountering a drunk on a shooting spree with a high-powered rifle. You know he will do more damage accidentally than he will intentionally, and if you patiently keep your distance, he will eventually shoot himself."

The Vols did eventually shoot themselves. One series of plays in the fourth quarter defined Tennessee's season. With just over six minutes remaining in a 3–3 game, Riggs scampered 23 yards off left tackle to the Alabama 4-yard line. The Vols were twelve feet from ripping control of the game away from Alabama, infuriating those sign-waving Alabama fans and knocking Auburn a little further into second place on the Tide's list of hated opponents. The critics said Riggs couldn't break a long run, but he did during one of the most crucial points of the season. The critics also said the often-injured Riggs would get hurt carrying the running load in 2005.

He did that, too.

Alabama cornerback Simeon Castille, the burly son of a former Tide star, fell awkwardly on Riggs' right lower leg as he pushed him out of bounds inside the 5. Riggs remained on the ground for several seconds near the Alabama bench. He pushed himself up, took a few steps, then crashed to the ground again. After overcoming his academic struggles, his bouts with immaturity, the long wait to become a starting running back and all those people who had written him off as a bust, Riggs' reward, on his longest run of the season, was significant ligament damage in his lower right calf and a fractured ankle.

"The guy fell on me and basically horse-collared me," said Riggs, who acknowledged the horse-collar tackle is legal in college football and didn't believe Castille meant to cause any harm. "He came down on the back of my ankle trying to tackle me. All of his weight came down on it. There was nothing I could do."

Karma, in this case, seemed delayed and unfair.

"It is baffling. It's a hard pill to swallow for us," his mother, Druann, said. "The only thing I am concerned about is how Gerald takes it. It's sad. It's frustrating. But he'll have to move forward from this. It's another learning experience. Gerald has proven he's a fighter."

Riggs dreamed of becoming the feature back at Tennessee like Jamal Lewis, Travis Henry, Charlie Garner and all of those other stars Riggs mentioned at the start of the season. He only got to experience his dream for six games. Riggs finished his career thirteenth on Tennessee's all-time rushing list with 1,893 yards despite starting just nine times. One of the most highly-coveted running backs coming out of high school, Riggs scored ten career touchdowns and was four yards short of No. 11.

Four very long yards. The season-defining drive wasn't over yet. On first down, Justin Reed reminded everyone the Vols do indeed use the tight end when he lifted his hand too early and was called for a false start. Following the penalty, redshirt freshman Arian Foster, in for Riggs, lost a yard on a carry, and the Vols were now at the 10-yard line. On second down, Clausen rolled right into wide-open space, kept jogging instead of bolting for the end zone, kept jogging, kept jogging, then threw the ball away after he crossed the line of scrimmage. It was the same corner of the end zone where his older brother, Casey, dove for the pylon and scored the game-winning touchdown in the fifth overtime against Alabama two years before. The quarterback who never made a mistake made a huge one. Five-yard penalty and a loss of down.

"I didn't want to force anything," Clausen explained later.

Only the Vols could turn first-and-goal from the 4 into third-and-goal from the 20 without a sack. Now Randy Sanders had a decision to make. He could call a conservative play, kick the field goal and pray John Chavis' defense could bail him out again. He could also take a shot at the end zone, and, if the play failed, the Vols would still be well within Wilhoit's range. Sanders had another idea: a screen pass to fullback Cory Anderson. Think about it. No one on the Tide defense would expect a screen pass to a 275-pound blocker, giving the Vols hope the play could turn into a touchdown. A screen pass is the safest throw in football. And there was no way Anderson, who is built like a linebacker, a position he played early in his career, would cough up the football. Sanders said he gleamed as he watched the play develop. Anderson caught the pass in plenty of space and followed blocks from Rob Smith, Cody Douglas and Richie Gandy. By the time Anderson reached the 5-yard line, he was a 275-pound bulldozer rolling downhill and prepared to level any poor soul wearing crimson who dared get in his way.

And that was the problem. Anderson, holding the ball high and tight in his right hand against his body, just as he'd been taught, was so focused on reaching the goal line that he never looked to his left to see talented Alabama safety Roman Harper take a pursuit angle that would make a geometry teacher proud. Harper put his helmet right on the football—a perfect tackle, Tennessee coaches would later say—to cause a fumble. The ball bounded out of the end zone. Touchback. Alabama football.

"I think Cory was a little surprised that a guy could get all the way across to the ball from the angle he was coming on," running backs coach Trooper Taylor said.

Southern Cal's Matt Leinart fumbles at the 3-yard line late in the fourth quarter against Notre Dame, and the ball rolls harmlessly out of bounds. Anderson fumbles the football at the 3-yard line, and it tumbles through the end zone. Welcome to Tennessee football, 2005. An offense of drunken hunters. Fulmer would later say a receiver was supposed to have blocked Harper on the play and simply didn't.

"We do some darn good things," Fulmer said, "and then we find a way to screw it up."

On third-and-9 following the fumble, Alabama's Brodie Croyle completed a 43-yard pass to receiver DJ Hall, who beat reserve cornerback Antonio Gaines, one of Jason Allen's replacements, down to the UT 35. "The receiver pushed off enough to make the catch, and that's what you've got to do," Chavis said, taking a veiled shot at the referees.

The week before, when the Crimson Tide blew out higher ranked Florida, Alabama officials said they had never heard Bryant-Denny Stadium so raucous and loud. However, the screaming of the home crowd reached a new fever pitch after Jamie Christensen booted a 34-yard field goal with thirteen seconds left to give Alabama a 6–3 lead over hated Tennessee. And like a bunch of drunken hunters, the Vols also committed a personal foul on the kickoff, and Fulmer put Ainge in the game to throw his second pass of the afternoon (he'd played one series earlier in the game with three freshmen receivers on the field) with eight seconds left. He threw an interception. Game over. The Evil Empire lay in ruins. Kevin Simon was wrong. The Vols were a .500 team.

Alabama fans belted out one of the loudest versions of "Rammer Jammer" ever heard inside Bryant-Denny Stadium, whipped out their lighters and, keeping with tradition in this rivalry, smoked celebratory cigars. Tennessee's season, meanwhile, went up in smoke, and Fulmer left the Bryant-Denny field to boos and vicious obscenities. During the post-game press conference in a plastic tent just outside the playing field, the cheers of Alabama fans were audible as a beaten Fulmer tried to convey his emotions over the sounds of those despised cheers.

Another figurative slap to an already red face.

The South Carolina Game:

"Get me through the third quarter, and I'll out-coach him in the fourth."

Steven Orr Spurrier, as the brash, witty, demanding coach of the wildly successful Florida Gators, seemingly took more pleasure in unleashing verbal jabs at opponents than the jabs he administered on the scoreboard. He did both quite frequently, winning an astonishing 122 games from 1990 to 2001 and delighting Gator booster clubs across the South with his clever insults concerning rival schools. He dubbed Florida State as "Free Shoes University" after police revealed Seminole players were getting mighty good discounts at a certain shoe store. He referred to former Georgia coach Ray Goff as "Ray Goof." When a fire burned 20 books at an Auburn University dorm, Spurrier exclaimed, "But the real tragedy was that 15 hadn't been colored yet!"

But Spurrier saved his best one-liners for Tennessee. Maybe it was because Spurrier, who had attended Science Hill High School in Johnson City, Tenn., wasn't recruited by the home-state Vols and went to Florida, where he won a Heisman Trophy as a quarterback. Maybe it was because Tennessee and Florida had ruled the SEC East in the nineties. Or maybe it was because the verbal barbs made beating Tennessee in those classic late-nineties battles that much more enjoyable. Whatever the reason, the infamous smirk on the face of "Steve Superior" glowed a little more when discussing Tennessee. Among his best:

- "You can't spell Citrus without *UT*," a reference to Tennessee's seemingly annual trips to the Citrus Bowl, which typically invited the SEC's second-best team, which was typically the Vols because, typically, they lost to Florida earlier in the season.
- "I know why Peyton came back for his senior year. He wanted to be a three-time Citrus Bowl MVP."
- Following the 1996 season, which had been a promising year for Phillip Fulmer's squad, Spurrier unveiled a sheet of Tennessee's goals. The first read, "National champions." Using a marker, Spurrier crossed it off. Florida reigned as national champions following a 52–20 rout of rival Florida State in the Sugar Bowl. The second read, "SEC champions." Another goal crossed out. The third read, "SEC East champions." That too, due to Florida's 35–29 win over Tennessee in Knoxville, did not materialize for the Vols, who once again made a familiar post-season trip to Orlando for the Citrus Bowl. The fourth goal read, "Tennessee state champions." Though winning a state title was not likely an objective for Fulmer in 1996, the Vols, ranked sixth nationally at the time, had indeed lost to unheralded Memphis 21–17. Another *X*. The fifth goal read, "Knox County champions."

  Spurrier circled it.

In his defense, Spurrier unleashed most of his taunts at Gator booster club meetings and his insults had spread through word of mouth. He didn't blast opponents in press conference settings, post-practice interviews or directly to anyone's face.

"At Florida State, they'd tell little corny jokes, we'd tell ours. Fans laugh, no big deal," Spurrier said. "But you tell one about Tennessee, and they think it's insulting or something. You'll never hear me complain about somebody telling a little, corny joke about our team."

Fulmer, who preferred to stay out of the media, did complain. "I didn't appreciate it," he said. "He has a different way sometimes when he gets a microphone in front of him."

But on April 13, 2005, after two years of silence, Spurrier launched his newest verbal jab from an unfamiliar location—South Carolina, where he had taken over for Lou Holtz following an unsuccessful stint in the NFL—and through an unfamiliar source: the media. Spurrier broke up the monotony of spring football by poking fun at the much-publicized flurry of arrests involving fight-happy Tennessee players. Spurrier downplayed an altercation involving South Carolina quarterback Syvelle Newton by comparing it with the recent aggravated assault charges filed against several Vols.

"This was not a full-blown fight. If you want to read about some full-blown fights, read about the Tennessee players, not our guys," Spurrier told The State newspaper in Columbia. "We've not had any knockdown, drag-out fights amongst our players."

In the past, Fulmer usually let Spurrier's taunts slide without a retort. Not this time, especially since nine current or former Gamecocks had been arrested in the previous four months.

"He needs to take care of his own house and leave mine to me, first of all," Fulmer said. "He's got plenty of issues over there

I'm sure to deal with. We've had a lot worse things than this that we've gotten through. I don't give a crap one way or the other what anybody says except the people that count."

Fulmer, a Tennessee grad who took the problems among players to heart because the school was so dear to him, was already fuming and embarrassed over the arrests. Now, here was an outsider—a rival!—making light of the situation. Fulmer went from steamed to pissed.

"He's got his own business, and he better be sure he's taking care of it," Fulmer said, his voice rising. "He's got plenty to do, I'm sure. Maybe it rained that day, and he didn't get to play golf. I don't know."

Fulmer then stormed off without taking anymore questions. Interview over.

And so it was official: Spurrier was back.

But his South Carolina squad certainly wouldn't resemble the intimidating machine he had assembled at Florida. The Gamecocks, who boasted just three bowl wins and one 10-win season dating back to 1892, finished 6–5 under Holtz in 2004. Under Spurrier, they fell at Georgia in his second game, lost to Alabama by 23 points at home and took a 48–7 beating at Auburn. But the Gamecocks were 4–3, the Vols were 3–3, and leave it to Spurrier to point that out.

"What's even stranger, I guess, is that before the season began, I think they were picked pretty much by most people to win the Eastern Division and maybe win the SEC," Spurrier said on his weekly teleconference. "Here we are—we're going into our eighth game, and they're going into their seventh, and we actually have a little bit of a better record than they do. Who would have thunk that before the season started?"

The answer was no one. Of course, no one figured the quarterback situation would still be unresolved. Sanders apologized to Ainge for playing him sparingly against Alabama, and Fulmer was now dodging questions concerning the quarterbacks. And the so-called best receivers in the conference were reacting to incoming passes like a soccer player trying to avoid a handball penalty. And the receivers were noticeably annoyed at Fulmer for singling them out—remember, he partly blamed the Anderson fumble on a receiver who missed a block on Roman Harper. So Fulmer took away their green no-contact practice jerseys to send a message they needed to get tougher. The receivers rolled their eyes.

"We don't hit in practice," said receiver Chris Hannon, who noted he preferred to wear his regular orange jersey anyway. "In a game, everything's full blow. Basically, I can put on the orange jersey. We don't go full contact. So it didn't stop anything. It's not going help anything. We're still 3–3, so it doesn't really even matter."

Amicable team manager Eric Haag says Fulmer is so competitive he'll turn friendly ping-pong games into all-day events until he wins. Fulmer doesn't handle losing well, and it was starting to show in his demeanor. He called Tennessee "the best 3–3 team in the nation" and blamed some of his team's problems on injuries, as if the Vols were the only ones to get hurt playing the game of football. While his players took to saying, "It is what it is," to describe their turmoil, Fulmer was still in full denial.

Again, an annoyed receiver: "Being 3–3 isn't an accomplishment," Jayson Swain said. "I don't know how to take that."

It is what it is.

Which was the exact sentiment toward the timing of the ceremony to retire Peyton Manning's number. The Indianapolis Colts' lone off weekend was October 29, the night Steve Spurrier would make his anticipated return to Neyland Stadium for the South Carolina-Tennessee game. The Vols couldn't even retire Manning's jersey without Spurrier in attendance, which prompted reminders that Manning had gone 0–4 against the Gators. It was like honoring the New York Yankees for winning the 2004 AL East title with the Boston Red Sox in attendance. So on a clear, mild Saturday night, the Vols retired Manning's No. 16 jersey—the same number worn by Rick Clausen—with Spurrier safely in the South Carolina locker room.

The revival of Tennessee's rivalry with Spurrier looked awfully familiar to Manning. Clausen switched jerseys to No. 7 for the game, but he looked a lot like No. 16 had against Spurrier back in the mid-nineties. On Tennessee's second possession, South Carolina's Johnathan Joseph picked off an errant Clausen pass at the UT 20-yard line. In the pre-season, Fulmer had said, "I told the quarterbacks not to look over their shoulders or start pressing." Following the interception, Fulmer yanked Clausen for Erik Ainge. Tennessee's quarterbacks weren't just looking over their shoulders at this point. They were peeking around offensive linemen toward the sideline and staring.

Ainge led a touchdown drive to tie the game 7–7 on his first possession, but completed one pass for negative yardage on a run-dominated second drive, which ended in a James Wilhoit field goal. Tennessee got the ball right back following a fumble on the kickoff, went backward two yards, Ainge missed a wide-open Swain in the end zone and then Wilhoit missed a 48-yard field goal. And if this is starting to sound familiar, wait until you hear what Arian Foster did at the goal line.

The Gamecocks—doing their best impression of Tennessee—fumbled again, this time at the UT 18 following a punt late in the second quarter with the Vols leading 12–7. Foster, an outstanding redshirt freshman running back who would prove to be more elusive and harder to bring down than Riggs, dragged tacklers on a third-and-1 run up the middle toward the goal line. Foster pumped his legs so furiously that he knocked the ball loose from his outstretched hand with his knee just before crossing the goal line. The ball fell at the feet of South Carolina's Stoney Woodson, who pounced on the loose ball in the end zone for a touchback.

Two games, two fumbles into the end zone.

"I was just trying to make a play," said Foster, who would carry the ball twenty-five times for 148 yards and a touchdown. "I made a mistake, the same kind of mistake that has been killing us all season."

Again, the drunken hunter offense.

Despite two fumbles on special teams, an interception thrown by Blake Mitchell at the UT 9 just before halftime and no semblance of the offense he ran at Florida, Spurrier, the Ol' Ball Coach, the nemesis of Fulmer and every Tennessee fan, somehow still had a chance. "Get me through the third quarter," one source said Spurrier told his team at halftime, "and I'll out-coach him in the fourth."

The Gamecocks got Spurrier through the third quarter without any change in the scoreboard. Perfect. All Spurrier had was one serious threat at wide receiver in redshirt freshman sensation Sidney Rice because Newton and Carlos Thomas were both out with injuries. Good enough. Spurrier hadn't beaten Fulmer seven out of ten times by accident. He always found a way. He was about to unload an array of pick routes on Tennessee to get Rice open. He was going to out-coach Fulmer in the fourth.

And on the first play of the fourth quarter, Rice caught a 28-yard pass in front of Antwan Stewart, going down at the Tennessee 19. After Spurrier used two straight timeouts to draw up a play, Rice caught a 5-yard touchdown pass to give the Gamecocks a 13–12 lead. Just get him through the third quarter, he had said. But sparked by a 23-yard run by Arian Foster, Tennessee reclaimed the lead, 15–13, on a 43-yard field goal by Wilhoit with 7:39 remaining.

But Spurrier kept his promise. He knew the Vols would adjust to the pick routes designed to get Rice, who now had eight catches for 112 yards, open over the middle. So he didn't throw to Rice at all. The drive started with a 13-yard pass from Mitchell to Kenny

McKinley, a five-foot-eleven former high school quarterback from Mableton, Ga. Tight end Kris Clark made his second catch of the game, a 15-yard grab, close to midfield. Another catch by Clark, for 10 yards. Another catch by McKinley, for 10 yards. Yet another catch by McKinley, this time for 7 yards. South Carolina marched all the way to Tennessee's 32-yard line without a single throw to Rice. Kicker Josh Brown booted a 49-yard field goal, the longest of his career, and South Carolina led 16–15 with 2:45 to go.

Fulmer, at last, sealed his loss in the coaching battle by reinserting Clausen—who had thrown three passes since his first-quarter interception—to run the two-minute drill. He completed three passes for 18 yards, and the Vols never crossed midfield. Different team, familiar result. Spurrier beat Fulmer again, spoiled Manning's big night and made his usual quips after the game. "I finally have a new line: 'God is smiling on the Gamecocks,'" Spurrier said. "That was the line I used after wins here when I was at Florida."

In his post-game analysis, colorful ESPN analyst Mark May had the following to say about the Spurrier-Fulmer rivalry: "It's like when you have a dog for ten years. You walk in the room, snap your fingers and say, 'Sit!' The dog immediately does what you tell him to do. That's what Steve Spurrier is to Phil Fulmer. Steve Spurrier absolutely owns Phil Fulmer."

Sit, Fulmer. Sit.

"He had the look on his face as if his wife and children had a car wreck," Spurrier told the Gamecock Club the following spring.

The Vols, now 3–4, were likely headed to a much different bowl than the Citrus that Spurrier joked about all the time.

After all, you can't spell Music City without UT.

The Notre Dame Game:

"A disastrous season."

As it turned out, the University of Tennessee picked a hell of a time to begin raising money to support Neyland Stadium's $107 million renovation project and to aid an athletic department on a tighter budget than a late-night Cinemax film. The dismissal of Tennessee basketball coach Buzz Peterson forced the athletic department to forsake its pride and borrow money from the university to pay off his $1.39 million buyout. Tennessee also paid new basketball coach Bruce Pearl $800,000, bought out his contract for $192,400 from Wisconsin-Milwaukee and paid Champ Search $25,000 to find him. The return of college football's 11-game schedule cost the Vols a seventh home game and $3.2 million more. Athletic director Mike Hamilton decided donations and funds from club seating sales would pay for the renovation project.

"We're in a belt-tightening time," Hamilton had noted in the spring of 2005.

Then the football team pulled the belt tighter by losing three straight games heading into a sure-fire disaster at red-hot Notre Dame, led by coach Charlie Weis. No one was real interested in handing out $250,000 up front and $32,000 per season for a club seat when the Vols couldn't even beat South Carolina at home. And they were still without an SEC title since 1998, no BCS appearances since 1999 and owned an 8–14 record against the conference's elite: Florida, Georgia, Auburn and LSU. Season ticket renewals would almost certainly decrease, Hamilton admitted donations would likely take a beating, and the $1 million he expected to earn from appearing in a BCS game was long forgotten. "In a year when the budget situation already wasn't rosy," Hamilton said, "a BCS bowl game would have been a nice bonus."

Hamilton was also paying Fulmer $2.05 million annually, and his buyout would exceed $4.6 million. But Hamilton refused to criticize Fulmer. He called the 2005 season a hiccup instead of an abberation and showed great support in one of the nation's winningest coaches.

"I'm very confident in Phillip," he said. "If I didn't know Phillip personally as well as I do, maybe I might not feel that way. Nobody works more hours than he does or puts in the time and effort. He has the right leadership skills and organizational skills. He has a concern for and loves the University of Tennessee. He's invested a lot of his life into this university. Success here means a lot to him."

Many fans disagreed. They rocked the message boards with criticism, vented their frustrations on radio talk shows and prompted quick hang-ups from Bob Kesling on Fulmer's weekly radio show, *Vol Calls*, for spewing insults at the head coach.

"I haven't kept up with the intensity of fan displeasure," Fulmer said. "I haven't picked up a newspaper. I'm sure there's a degree of frustration. But it's amazing the amount of cards and letters in support, and on *Vol Calls* people are supportive. If you watched the games, it's pretty easy to be frustrated like we are that we haven't won the games, but it's not like we've gone in and gotten our rear ends blown out anywhere. We've been in positions to win the ball games and just haven't gotten it done."

But with a win at No. 8 Notre Dame, maybe the Vols could improve morale and their post-season chances. Maybe they would relish the opportunity to get one more chance to beat a ranked team and regain some respect. Maybe Erik Ainge, the full-time starter once again, would learn from his forgettable start to the season and return to the form he had shown a year ago. Maybe Tennessee's stout defense could slow down Notre Dame's high-powered offense and score just enough against a weak defense to pull off an upset.

Or maybe the Vols would neatly put together all of the season's screw-ups into one nice package and put them on display, so Notre Dame Stadium and an NBC television audience unfamiliar with Tennessee football could catch up on recent events. A *CliffsNotes* of the season, if you will.

Bad special teams? Check. Freshman Lucas Taylor fumbled during a kickoff return to set up Notre Dame's second touchdown. The Vols also allowed Tom Zbikowski to sprint through the middle of the field almost untouched for a 78-yard punt return to give Notre Dame a 21–3 lead in the second quarter.

Bad third-and-long defense? Check. Tied 21–21 and facing

third-and-10 from the Notre Dame 25, Brady Quinn completed a short pass over the middle to Jeff Samardzija, who sprinted past a stumbling Jonathan Wade for 73 yards down to the two. On third-and-goal, Samardzija hauled in a touchdown pass to give the Irish a 28–21 lead.

Bad quarterback play? Check. Following Samardzija's touchdown, Notre Dame's Ambrose Wooden intercepted one of Ainge's patented forced passes to set up a field goal. Ainge, also called for intentional grounding twice in the game—the kid plain refuses to take a sack—threw his final interception by severely underthrowing Jayson Swain. As Zbikowski ran back the interception 33 yards for a touchdown to give Notre Dame a 41–21 lead, Fulmer walked down the sideline with his head down. He put his hands on his knees and stared at the ground.

Defeated. Again. The Vols were on their first four-game losing streak in seventeen years and finally finished the stages of going through a horrendous season. Forgive the Vols if they were slow to learn. Their last losing season was in 1988, and their five losses matched the number of games they dropped in the 1995, 1996, 1997 and 1998 seasons combined.

The four stages of losing at a big-time program: denial, hope, frustration and, following the 41–21 loss to Notre Dame, acceptance.

"A disastrous season," right guard Cody Douglas said. "That's what it is. It's a disaster."

Said Arron Sears: "It's like a bad dream."

Even linebacker Kevin Simon, who had boldly stated earlier

in the season the Vols weren't a .500 team—he was right, they were worse—finally concluded the Vols, in short, stunk.

"I can't figure out what's going on," he said.

Three winnable games still remained on Tennessee's schedule—Memphis, Vanderbilt and Kentucky. The Vols were 60–1 in their last 61 combined meetings against those teams, and three wins would guarantee them a spot in a bottom-tier bowl game. Their chances of playing in the postseason were still favorable. The fans were even done making the offensive coordinator's wife and children cry.

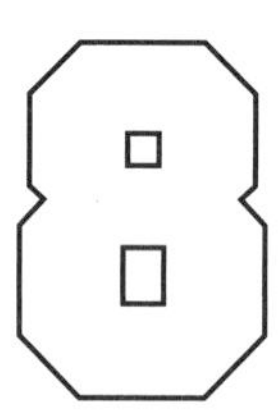

Randy Sanders Resigns

RANDY SANDERS KISSED the dark hair of his wife, Cathy, a friendly woman with an unmistakable laugh, and whispered into her ear. She was crying. Sanders looked down at the red eyes of his two beautiful preteen daughters, Kelly and Kari, and attempted to offer a comforting smile. Fresh off hearing fans unleash a verbal tirade aimed at their father as they headed toward the interview room, they had already asked Mommy if they could miss school Monday.

"A kid once came up to my oldest daughter and said, 'Your dad sucks,'" Sanders said. "That's tough for any child."

By the time Sanders wheeled around to face the media following Tennessee's 16–15 loss to South Carolina, he already knew his next move once the last reporter left the post-game interview room.

He would resign as Tennessee's offensive coordinator.

Sanders could handle the criticism. He could handle insults hurled his way. But he couldn't handle his family in tears following games. "I have to take my share," he said. "I just wish my wife and kids didn't have to deal with it."

The offensive coordinator's position at Tennessee is a thankless job, and he knew it. The popular Phillip Fulmer was almost immune to verbal assaults, though in 2005 his status among fans was rapidly changing. Long-time defensive coordinator John Chavis, the gruff, fierce former walk-on at Tennessee known as "Chief," commanded respect and was revered by fans because of his success, particularly in big games. Even when the defense struggled at times in 2004, fans aimed their venom at defensive backs coach Larry Slade.

That leaves the offensive coordinator to handle the brunt of the criticism. Tennessee fans clamored for former Ole Miss coach David Cutcliffe to return as offensive coordinator when the Vols started struggling in 2005, but when he departed before the 1998 national championship game, they weren't exactly blocking the moving trucks to prevent him from leaving. Sports information director Bud Ford once waited at the Tennessee tunnel just before halftime of a game so he could chastise Cutcliffe, one of the most successful coordinators in Tennessee history, as he headed toward the locker room. Cutcliffe responded by cursing him out. And Sanders certainly had his own criticism to endure. There was a firerandysanders.com website, and someone at the Knoxville Quarterback Club showed off a T-shirt that read, "Randy Sanders Dating Service: Guaranteed Not To Score."

The offensive coordinator at Tennessee is the punching bag, the redheaded stepchild, the fall guy.

And Sanders took the fall.

Sanders' Halloween announcement that he would trick-or-treat for another job following the season didn't surprise those closest to the witty, easygoing, born-and-raised Tennessean, who felt most comfortable with a fishing rod in his hand. Several signs throughout the season indicated that Sanders knew his seven-year run as offensive coordinator was in jeopardy and, at times, his desire to coach was waning. During Tennessee's media day following the win at LSU, a reporter asked Sanders how many banged-up offensive linemen had been in question to play in the second half.

"After the first half," Sanders said, "I'm in question."

Friends claim Sanders lost his desire to coach following the 6–3 loss to Alabama. The game plan against the Tide, Sanders would later say, was to play a low-scoring, field position game and try to win the thing at the end. As Cory Anderson rumbled toward the end zone late in the fourth quarter, the plan seemed to be working just fine. But Anderson fumbled, Alabama scored, and Sanders knew the backlash was going to be more severe than ever before. His two daughters, ages twelve and nine, began asking to miss school, which prompted Fulmer to admit his oldest daughter, Courtney, had once confronted a bully at school for ridiculing her father.

"She pinned a young man against the locker for something he said about me," Fulmer said. "We had to go to the school and talk about it. I couldn't condone it. It's like I tell our players, you have to walk away. But I didn't completely disagree with it, either."

Rumors began floating around that Fulmer would overhaul the offensive coaching staff at the end of the season—receivers coach Pat Washington's wife, Claudette, was telling friends they were all but listing their house for sale—and following the loss to South Carolina, it was Fulmer who said, "We'll make whatever tough decisions that need to be made and whatever personnel looks that need to be made." He could have been talking about changing the starting lineup. Or, more likely, he was talking about changing some faces on the sideline.

The last Tennessee coach to lose a game to South Carolina, Johnny Majors, was forced out of his job six days later in 1992. Sanders didn't wait that long and didn't allow Fulmer to decide his fate. During his conversation with reporters following the South Carolina game, Sanders kept talking about a "long, tough meeting" that needed to take place the following day. He thanked the reporters, found Fulmer and said he wanted to resign. Fulmer, admittedly shocked, told Sanders to sleep on the thought and meet with him the next day. The two spoke at great length Sunday, and Sanders didn't budge. He would resign his offensive coordinator's job immediately, stay on as quarterbacks coach for the rest of the season and then, for the first time in twenty-two years, spend a football season away from the University of Tennessee. On

Monday morning, he told the quarterbacks, then the rest of the team in an emotional meeting later in the afternoon before facing the media.

In 2004, Sanders groomed two freshmen quarterbacks and a journeyman third-string junior, and helped Tennessee to the SEC title game with high-scoring wins over Vanderbilt and Kentucky. The Vols posted twenty-eight points against undefeated and defensive-minded Auburn, then scored thirty-eight in the Cotton Bowl against Texas A&M. When fall camp began, Fulmer said no assistant in the country had done a better job than Sanders in 2004.

Three months later, Fulmer accepted his resignation. Ironically, it was Fulmer who'd called Ole Miss's firing of Cutcliffe "a travesty," simply because he'd suffered through one troubling season. Now, changes on Fulmer's own offensive staff were occurring before the season was even over. College football can be a cruel, unforgiving sport.

Sanders announced his resignation publicly in the very same room where he typically leaned against a white folding table during Tennessee's Tuesday media day and answered every question honestly, directly and with his unique sense of humor. On this Monday, October 31, Sanders faced the media with a red face and a quivering voice. He nearly broke down in tears several times early in the press conference but never lost his composure.

"If I'm going to put in fourteen- and sixteen-hour days for six days and get the results we've got, that's not what I need," he said. "Somewhere along the line, things have gotten out of kilter a little bit offensively this year. I don't necessarily know that it's all my fault. The fact is, it's my ship."

Sanders' ship sank quickly in 2005, ranking 108th out of 117 Division I teams nationally in scoring offense at 16.1 points per game. The Vols, who Sanders said had "all the pieces" for a prolific offense in the pre-season, also ranked 99th in total offense, 98th in rushing offense and 101st in passing efficiency. Students had chanted "fire Randy Sanders" at the end of Tennessee's loss to South Carolina.

"I'm going to miss this place," he said. "The fact is, there's a whole lot more to life than Tennessee football. I think the last few weeks have brought me to that realization. It's not just a spur-of-the-moment decision. I'm not going to sit around and say that I've been thinking about doing this for the whole season, either. That's not the case. But why wait? Coach Fulmer has been great about this. It wasn't something he approached me with. It wasn't something anybody else approached me with. I came to him with it. I have never believed in beating around the bush. I've always tried to treat the quarterbacks and the players and anybody else I've dealt with in a very straightforward manner. I tell them all the time, 'I'll tell you the truth. It might not be what you want to hear, but I'll tell you the truth.' Where I am right now is the truth. So why wait? This isn't a response to criticism. This is a response to what I'm seeing on the field."

Even at his lowest point and fighting back tears, Sanders still couldn't resist firing off a final one-liner and making the "suits"—members of the administration lingering in the back of the room—squirm a little more. Sanders, who once said he hoped his freshmen quarterbacks would play like a great Christmas present instead of "that third crockpot," snickered as he answered one final question.

"I'm not resigning to keep from getting fired. The best thing in the world to happen to me is to get fired. Then, I get my full contract," he said.

In the back of the room, members of Tennessee's athletic department—particularly associate athletics director Carmen Tegano—motioned for the press conference to end and threw a fit once the room cleared. They didn't want Sanders answering too many questions anyway, and now he was talking money and his contract. Press conference over.

Sanders, still looking beaten down, still angry at the abuse his family had taken and still emotional following the press conference, still managed a smile. The fall guy had one final laugh.

Rick Clausen wasn't laughing. UT officials didn't allow player interviews following Sanders' announcement, but they permitted the captains to speak on Tuesday. Clausen was one of the six captains. And, man, he was ready to talk. He was pumped. Clausen seemed to take the perceived backlash from fans more personally than anyone—he'd ridiculed them after the Ole Miss game and all but disowned them following the Georgia loss—and now he had the perfect forum on which to unload.

"The fans started pointing fingers, the media started pointing fingers, and it's so unfortunate it had to be Coach Sanders, but hey, I guess that's the person people around here like to pick on," Clausen said. "Not only are you affecting him, but you're affecting his family and affecting his kids. That's not right. We're supposed to be the Tennessee family, and you're just going to kick him to the curb like that. That ain't right. This is a so-called family, so let's act like a family. It's just disheartening that everyone claims to be part of the Tennessee family and the Vol Nation. But at the first sign of adversity, everybody decides to blame Coach Sanders."

Clausen didn't limit his criticism to the fans. Clausen, along with the other offensive players who'd made key mistakes in the red zone in close games, were traumatized by Sanders' announcement and felt responsible for his resignation. Even Fulmer said he wasn't sure Sanders would be resigning if the Vols hadn't fumbled three times inside the 10-yard line, which certainly wasn't Sanders' fault. Just two days before, Clausen's awful first-quarter interception had set up South Carolina's first touchdown, and he'd only managed one first down on the Volunteers' potential game-winning drive.

"I'm just pissed at the whole situation. I'm pissed at everybody. I'm pissed at myself," Clausen said. "I feel like I let him down. His job and his wife's livelihood and his daughters' livelihood were basically in my hands. If I go out and don't throw an interception, we probably beat South Carolina. If I don't throw an interception against Georgia, we probably beat Georgia. If we don't fumble the ball two times inside the 10-yard line against Alabama, we probably beat Alabama, and nobody's talking about this right now. That's the most upsetting thing. The players have done it. The players have basically forced Coach Sanders to resign."

So had pressure from the fans. Clausen, offensive guard Cody Douglas and center Rob Smith—the only offensive players available to the media on that Tuesday—acknowledged that some fans, without being specific, had verbally abused Sanders and his family this year aside from the South Carolina game. They could hear it from the stands. Before the season, Sanders had said he would consider getting out of the game if he couldn't separate family and football. It had happened. The players had heard it.

"Obviously, he's fallen under a lot of pressure from the people around here, like fans," Douglas said. "The one thing I wish I could do, I wish I could go to some of these people's jobs and criticize them whenever they do something wrong or whenever somebody under them does something wrong that may not necessarily be their fault. I wish I could hold open forum on them and bash them. But I can't do that."

Bashing fans. A pissed-off quarterback. Resigning coordinators. Crying children.

This is what 2005 had become for Tennessee football.

"It's a bunch of crap," Clausen said.

A bunch of crap.

So crudely stated and yet so wonderfully accurate. Four words couldn't describe Tennessee's season any better. A bunch of crap.

And then a funny thing happened in the aftermath of Sanders' resignation. There was no celebration. There was no sign of relief. Newspaper columnists didn't support the move. There was no attitude among the fans that their team's offense would take off following Sanders' exit as play-caller. Tennessee fans had clamored for Sanders' dismissal for three years, finally got their wish and then pouted some more. It was like a kid asking for a bike for Christmas, waking up to a shiny new red Radio Flyer by the tree, then complaining he didn't get a go-cart. Posters on message boards, where Sanders took the most heat, suddenly agreed Sanders probably wasn't at fault and receivers coach Pat Washington should go. Maybe offensive line coach Jimmy Ray Stephens should go. Why stop on offense? Slade can't seem to coach up the defensive backs, he should go as well. Typical hard-to-please Tennessee fans.

The general consensus among the media and fans was this: Sanders had taken the fall for Fulmer's aging offense and ridiculous quarterback rotation. He'd basically fallen on a sword sharpened by criticism. In a survey of *Chattanooga Times Free Press* readers, only 4.1 percent blamed Tennessee's woes on Sanders. More than sixty percent blamed Fulmer.

John Adams, the witty columnist for the *Knoxville News-Sentinel*, wrote this about Fulmer: "Everybody should have a job like this: You make $2 million a year; when things go well, you get praise and a raise; when things go bad, someone else takes the fall. Tennessee offensive coordinator Randy Sanders took the fall."

Parents were upset, and not just any parents. Jim Clausen, the father of Rick Clausen and, more importantly, high school quarterback phenom Jimmy Clausen, fumed at Sanders' apparently forced resignation. Not even the immediate rumors that

Cutcliffe, who had developed Peyton and Eli Manning, would take over for Sanders could make Clausen and Doug Ainge feel any better. Privately, the fathers of Tennessee's two quarterbacks groaned about Fulmer's rotation.

"I'm sure they'll come at us with David Cutcliffe, if they get him, and say he's all the things Randy wasn't," Jim Clausen said. "But you look at how some things have been handled. Really, what will be different for Jimmy?"

David and Janet Crompton, the parents of highly recruited freshman quarterback Jonathan Crompton, drove to Knoxville from their home in Waynesville, N.C. that Monday to hear the news themselves and comfort Sanders. "It's a very bad day," David Crompton said. "A lot of Tennessee fans don't realize Randy Sanders is a heck of a guy and a heck of a football coach. The program lost a lot. Our family is pretty emotional. I'm not saying Jonathan is not going to work like heck, because he will. But the program lost a great football coach."

Fans did take some satisfaction knowing Cutcliffe would be the man. Everybody knew that. Fulmer acted as though he wanted to conduct a nationwide search for Sanders' replacement, knowing the whole time the answer was already in Knoxville. Cutcliffe moved to Knoxville in 2005 after he resigned June 1 as Notre Dame's quarterbacks coach due to ongoing heart problems. Cutcliffe had landed the job at Notre Dame after six years at Ole Miss, where he'd won SEC Coach of the Year honors in 2003 but was stunningly fired following a 4–7 season in 2004, as if the historically mediocre Rebels were accustomed to ten-win seasons. Cutcliffe's son, Chris, was already working as a student manager for the Vols.

"Who knows what the future holds?" Cutcliffe said. "I'd like to be a head football coach. I'm not trying to be arrogant, but I hope the opportunity presents itself. If not, I'd never rule out coming back to Tennessee."

Cutcliffe said he wanted to wait and apply for head coaching vacancies before committing to Fulmer, but Kentucky announced it was holding onto Rich Brooks despite another poor season, and Texas Tech's Mike Leach, a hot name in coaching circles, said he wasn't going anywhere. Fulmer said he wanted to wait and review the applications he received, but no one had Cutcliffe's credentials or his strong relationship with Fulmer. Cutcliffe had even picked Fulmer to be in his wedding party. With Cutcliffe as offensive coordinator from 1993 to '98, the Vols had led the SEC in total offense three times, rushing offense three times and scoring offense once. They finished 63–11 over that span. And Fulmer trusted Cutcliffe. He was loyal to Cutcliffe. Fulmer had blasted Ole Miss after letting Cutcliffe go and made the snide comment about Ed Orgeron following the Tennessee-Ole Miss game.

"At an appropriate time, when we get things going better, and I have time to think through it, David will certainly be one of the people that I'll talk to," Fulmer said.

Less than a month later, Fulmer would hire Cutcliffe.

Meanwhile, Sanders, who had spent more than half of his life—twenty-two out of forty years—at Tennessee, mulled a life without coaching, regretted not spending more time with the quarterbacks, spent rare time with his family in the normally hectic recruiting month of December, and told the Tennessee Football Coaches Association at its winter clinic, "Don't worry about walking out on me. When you've been booed by 110,000 people, believe me, you won't hurt my feelings."

Everyone laughed.

Sanders, of course, also spent an inordinate amount time of fishing.

"My wife looked at me the other day and said I was getting fat," he told the *Knoxville News-Sentinel.* "So I told her I was going on a new workout regimen. I would stand up when I fish."

Randy Sanders. The fall guy. The funny guy. The family guy. My favorite assistant.

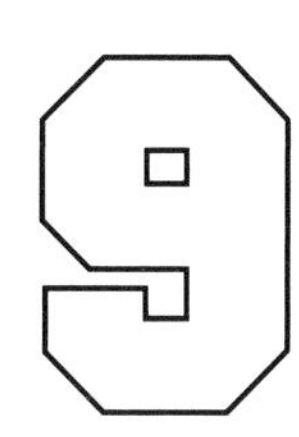

Hitting Rock Bottom

VANDERBILT: *noun*, 1. An independent, privately supported university in Nashville, Tenn. 2. The laughingstock of SEC football, posting a 7–73 conference record from 1995 to 2004 and winning exactly one bowl game in school history. *verb,* 3. To inexplicably, suddenly, yet predictably implode during any pivotal moment or when a ray of positive hope creeps into the program; often used with "to pull—" as in, "To pull a Vanderbilt."

Football fields are one hundred yards long, goal line to goal line. Ten yards makes a first down. Touchdowns are six points. Tennessee beats Vanderbilt.

Such are the seemingly permanent rules of college football. Entering their 2005 meeting at Neyland Stadium, the Vols owned a twenty-two-game winning streak against the Vanderbilt Commodores—the second-longest stretch of domination over one opponent behind Notre Dame's annual beating of Navy—and hadn't lost to the Commodores at home since 1975. The Commodores had been scoreless in Neyland Stadium since 1999 and had failed to score more than fourteen points in a game at Tennessee since 1987. The last Vandy quarterback to beat Tennessee, Whit Taylor in 1982, is still a legend in Nashville.

But very few people believed, despite all their travails in 2005, that the Vols would actually lose to Vanderbilt on the afternoon of November 19. Chris Low, the talented, veteran beat writer for *The Tennessean*, argued that the Vols would almost certainly screw up one of their last three games, either against Memphis, Vanderbilt or Kentucky even though the Vols had won sixty of sixty-one games against those teams. He predicted they would fail to make a bowl game for the first time since 1988. But not even Low could bring himself to pick Vanderbilt over the Vols, who were fourteen-point favorites.

Not that the Vols were giving anyone a reason to believe they could beat anybody. They almost fulfilled Low's prophecy against Memphis, an average Conference USA team playing without superstar running back DeAngelo Williams (ankle sprain) and using a wide receiver at quarterback because of injuries to the previous three signal callers.

But even Memphis had to snicker at Tennessee's quarterback situation, which had changed again—at this point, it was becoming laughable—when Erik Ainge suffered a complete meltdown to start the game. He threw two interceptions in four passes—officials called one back because of a late-hit penalty—and finished one of three for six yards. The Vols fell behind 13–0 in the second quarter before Rick Clausen cleaned up the mess with two touchdown passes in six minutes before halftime, and players began openly imploring for Clausen to get more playing time following the 20–16 win.

"It's been evident to everybody that the offense just flows a little better with Rick in the game," receiver C.J. Fayton said.

Added receiver Chris Hannon, "If I was Ainge, my confidence would be pretty low."

Even former quarterback Brent Schaeffer, who had left the team in the spring of 2005 to the delight of the UT coaches annoyed with his constant tardiness, troubles with the law, bad attitude, insistence on smoking cigarettes and poor grades, piled on Ainge from his junior college in California.

"I think if I was there they would be a good team," Schaeffer told the *Visalia* (Calif.) *Times-Delta*. "They don't have the right player in the spot they need—the person to make the big plays ... I felt like I was the best quarterback there."

During Vanderbilt week, reserve offensive lineman Ell Ash, another player known for his rotten attitude, launched into an obscenity-laced outburst at his coaches and teammates during practice. By now, Ash's bad behavior was hardly news, he had been present at the infamous nightclub brawl the week of the 2004 SEC championship game. But Ash picked a bad time to unleash these curse words. He said them right in front of athletic director Mike Hamilton, who was attending practice that day and watched the scene unfold from the sideline.

Fulmer kicked Ash off the team.

The Vols were still the Vols.

But the Commodores were pulling Vanderbilts at an alarming rate, even by their standards. They stunned the college football world by starting the season 4–0, including a road win against Arkansas. All they needed was a win over hapless Sun Belt nobody Middle Tennessee State to go an astounding 5–0, pull within one victory of becoming bowl-eligible and set up a nationally televised showdown at home against LSU.

ESPN switched to the game just in time to air the final seconds of Vanderbilt's inexplicable—yet, as the definition goes, somewhat predictable—17–15 loss to MTSU, a team that played so poorly in 2005, the school fired coach Andy McCollum at the end of the season.

Pulled a Vanderbilt.

The Commodores went on to lose badly to LSU and Georgia, then gave up a late touchdown in a loss to South Carolina and dropped the idea of attempting a two-point conversion trailing by a single point at Florida when receiver Earl Bennett was flagged for unsportsmanlike conduct after a late touchdown. The Commodores lost in overtime.

Yep, pulled two more Vanderbilts.

The week before playing Tennessee, the Commodores figured to pound a horrible Kentucky team at home to at least set up a chance to become bowl-eligible. Representatives of the Music City Bowl in Nashville even spoke excitedly of hosting the hometown Commodores if they could get to six wins. Almost on cue as the bowl talk started, Vanderbilt fell behind 34–10 at halftime and lost by five. In 2004—a season full of Vanderbilts—the Commodores lost five games by a total of fifteen points and were outscored 81–20 after the third quarter. But in 2005 they were competing. At least they had hope. Now, a six-game losing streak officially erased any post-season chances for the twenty-third straight year.

Pulled a Vanderbilt.

But the Vols were about to pull a Vanderbilt of their own.

Very few people around the Tennessee program could honestly say they saw it coming. Everyone knew some unrest existed in the program, the quarterback situation was a mess, Vanderbilt was capable of scoring points, and Tennessee was not. But all the players were handling themselves the right way. Rob Smith, the intelligent, easygoing offensive lineman from Kentucky who'd taken Arabic courses, wanted to be either in the secret service or a grade-school teacher and never missed a media day, swore none of the defensive players were giving members of the offense hell for essentially ruining the season.

"If I were them," Smith said, "I probably would."

For selfish reasons or not, the players also seemed sincere about keeping Tennessee's post-season streak alive. Lose to Vanderbilt, and the Vols were assured of their first sub-.500 season since 1988. Lose, and Tennessee's sixteen-year bowl streak—the third longest in the nation behind Michigan (30) and Florida State (23)—would be over. Lose, and Tennessee's players would be forever regarded as the talented group who couldn't even make the post-season.

"If we lose, we're going to be singing the tune, 'I'll Be Home for Christmas,'" center David Ligon said. "We don't want to be home for Christmas. We don't want to be remembered as the Tennessee team that didn't go to a bowl game. If that's not enough motivation for you, then you don't need to be playing football at Tennessee. I mean, that would be our legacy."

A senior-laden defense, which was holding the team together, said they simply wouldn't allow Vanderbilt to beat them on Senior Day. No way. Mature seniors on defense—and remember, these guys are playing under the fierce John Chavis—like Jesse Mahelona, Jason Hall, Kevin Simon, Omar Gaither and Parys Haralson would rather give up 200 rushing yards to a freshman running back than exit Neyland Stadium for the final time as losers to Vanderbilt. And redshirt freshman Arian Foster, a third-string tailback earlier in the season, was turning into a legitimate star, averaging 136.5 yards rushing in his lone two career starts. Surely he would treat a poor Vanderbilt defense like a row of tackling dummies. "Arian has some of the best vision I've seen from any back I've blocked for here," senior right guard Cody Douglas said.

And then there was the astonishing, moving, almost unbelievable story of senior linebacker Jason Mitchell.

Throughout the season, Mitchell offered the same response when asked about his ailing left knee. It couldn't get any worse, he would say, then force a smile. Three years ago, the reporters would have shaken their heads and wondered what exactly Mitchell was talking about. When he arrived at Tennessee in 2002, Mitchell was not at all media savvy. He cursed during interviews, made nonsensical statements and generally was the worst quote on the team.

It turned out he'd just been shy and a little nervous. Mitchell matured over the years, became one of the team leaders and morphed into a media favorite, though he still did not like answering questions in front of TV cameras. They made him nervous, he said. But he rarely ducked Tuesday's media day, a common practice among the Vols during difficult times, and would lean against a desk counter, answer questions eloquently and even add his own brand of humor. Asked if he would rather face a mobile quarterback with poor arm strength or a stationary quarterback with a great arm, it was Mitchell who said, with a straight face, he would rather face a stationary quarterback with no arm strength. He paused, then laughed along with the reporters. He became a go-to guy for writers in need of a quote.

So when Mitchell ducked questions about his left knee, the beat writers suspected there was more to the story.

We had no idea.

Someone asked Mitchell how much the knee limited him. He laughed.

"Well, a lot actually," he said. "I may be like a third of myself out there trying to play. It's crazy. I shouldn't have been playing at all, and this is going to be my last game as a Vol."

What?

"I should have stopped playing around the Georgia game," he said.

Huh?

Mitchell finally relented. On the Tuesday before Tennessee faced Vanderbilt, Mitchell admitted he had played almost the entire season with a torn ACL and MCL in his left knee, putting his future NFL career at risk. After the Vanderbilt game, he would finally walk away, satisfied he put in all the effort he could into the Tennessee football program. But not before jogging through the *T* inside Neyland Stadium on Saturday and absorbing the college football atmosphere he loved so much for the final time as a player. He'd gaze out at the orange-clad fans who had supported him for four years, embrace teammates, put on his helmet and start at middle linebacker when Tennessee hosted Vanderbilt. The following day, he would fly to California and undergo season-ending knee surgery on Monday.

"It's my love for the game, my love for my teammates. I didn't want to leave on somebody else's terms," he said. "I wanted to leave when I felt I was ready. I wasn't ready to fold up the tent my senior year, even though it could have hurt me in the long run, which it probably might. I just enjoyed the time and loved it. My love for the game, my love for my teammates, my love for playing for the university kept me still playing."

After hearing the news, fellow linebacker Kevin Simon called

Mitchell "crazy." As a two-year starter, an NFL career almost certainly awaited Mitchell, who tore the ligaments in Tennessee's season opener against UAB but didn't find out the severity of the injury until two days before the Georgia game. Instead of undergoing surgery and starting the rehabilitation process in time to prepare for the NFL combine, Mitchell said he felt strong enough to play the rest of the season even though his knee, held together by a brace, shook violently each time he absorbed a hit. The pain was almost unbearable. An MRI showed his ACL was in shreds. His knee wiggled like jelly when he moved laterally.

Mitchell's family met with Tennessee coaches and members of the medical staff once an MRI determined his ligaments were torn instead of sprained, as the initial diagnosis had erroneously suggested. They tried to explain to Mitchell the long-term risks of playing on a torn ACL.

"I said, 'Hey, if it was me, I would not play,'" Chavis said. "I didn't want to tell him that he couldn't play. I appreciate what he has done, but I probably would not have played had it been me."

Teammates were blunt; said they thought he was stupid. Mitchell heard the criticism many times from fellow players, friends and his brother, former NFL lineman Brandon Mitchell. He was risking his career for a 4–5 team.

"It's still just actually playing and living out a dream that you wanted to do, and that's bigger than the NFL," he said. "To me, I got to the point now where I can finally walk away. I can finally play the game and walk away from it being comfortable. Before, I couldn't do that. It's still my life and my body. Once they tell you what's wrong and you make a decision after that, it's your decision. They cannot tell you how to live your life. You can't tell a person with cancer to do chemo even if they don't want to. It was the same thing with me. I didn't want to do it. I didn't want to stay out.

"The NFL is not guaranteed at all. That's a chance you take. And to play a game at this level and live your dream out is something that you can't get back at all. I said I would play this game and play as long as I can. I know surgery might not get me to play football again, but it will get me to walk. And as long as I enjoyed the time here, the now, I'm more into enjoying the now than hoping for a future that might not even be there."

He's crazy. He's stupid. He just wants to walk. He's Jason Mitchell, an Abbeville, La., native who works at a foundation he and his brother started seven years ago to help underprivileged families and who spent one of his off weekends loading trucks with supplies for Hurricane Katrina victims. At the time, he didn't tell anyone he was loading those trucks on a dismantled knee. He recorded thirty-one tackles in 2005—way below expectations—but didn't tell anyone in the media he was less than fifty percent healthy.

"You don't really know what to say," Gaither said. "It just shows you how much he cares about this team and the program that he was willing to suffer through that all season when he could have gotten surgery earlier. We don't have the best record in the world, but he still played for us, and he still went out there and gave us his all. He's Jason Mitchell. That's the way he is."

Surely the Vols wouldn't lose after such an emotional admission from one of the team's leaders. If Mitchell could play on a shredded knee, the Vols could sure as hell try to win two games against two poor teams. Mitchell's story provided a break in the monotony of negative stories, backlash and frustration of the season. The Vols finally had a reason to be proud. The guy had all but thrown away his entire NFL career to play on Senior Day. They had to win.

Plus, it was Vanderbilt. Freaking Vanderbilt.

And in the second quarter, the Vols were losing to freaking Vanderbilt 21–7.

Same old story: two penalties on the Vols keyed two Vanderbilt touchdown drives, and the secondary seemed almost determined to make quarterback Jay Cutler a first-round pick before the final whistle blew. His first NFL contract was growing more expensive with every pass. But Rick Clausen, who beat Erik Ainge in a spirited game of rock-paper-scissors to earn the starting job against Vandy (is it that unbelievable?), threw a late first-half touchdown to Chris Hannon, and the Vols trailed 21–14 at halftime.

Bobby Johnson told his team, "Get me through the third quarter, and I'll outcoach him in the fourth." Okay, so he didn't mimic Spurrier's halftime line, but the Commodores did indeed get Johnson through the third quarter without any change on the scoreboard. And that was a problem. When you're famous for having fourth quarter collapses named in honor of your team, no lead is ever large enough. The Commodores could blow a seven-point lead with ease.

And on the first play of the fourth quarter, right on cue, Arian Foster rumbled into the end zone on third-and-goal to tie the score. On the Commodores' first possession of the quarter, Cutler took a sack, and they netted just 17 yards on the punt. Tennessee took over at the Vanderbilt 37 and kicked a field goal to take a 24–21 lead with 8:25 remaining.

Typical Vanderbilt.

The final five minutes featured a ferocious, cutthroat battle between two teams trying their hardest to blow the game. The Vols just needed one—one!—first down in their final two possessions to all but put the game away. Following a Vanderbilt punt, typical play-not-to-lose Fulmer called three straight Foster runs and failed to get a first down. Tennessee punted. The Commodores went backward seven yards and, surprisingly, punted the ball right back to Tennessee with just 2:22 remaining. Johnson, who had all three timeouts left, was basically betting the game on the assumption that the Vols couldn't get a first down against his outmanned, weary defense.

He was right. Foster carried for two yards. Timeout, Vanderbilt. Foster carried for three yards. Timeout, Vanderbilt. Now Vandy senior linebacker Herdley Harrison, a bright young man from Marietta, Ga., had not bitten on any misdirections or reverse plays the entire game. As a senior should, especially a senior at one of the South's most prestigious universities, he always stayed at home and remained in his gap. And so when Fulmer called a reverse to freshman Lucas Taylor on third-and-5, Harrison was not fooled. He waited for Taylor, then stuffed him for no gain. The Vols had to punt.

Cutler, the gritty, tough quarterback from Santa Claus, Ind., playing in his final collegiate game, was getting one more chance. One final drive in his college career. One moment Cutler, who was 10–34 with the Commodores, could relish instead of regret.

Come on, like he was going to pull a Vanderbilt.

It's amazing how a miserable twenty-two-year streak could end so simply and easily. With 1:40 remaining, Cutler started the drive with a 15-yard pass across the middle to the sensational freshman receiver Earl Bennett, who was covered by Tennessee's Inky Johnson, down to the UT 48-yard line.

"On the last series," Vanderbilt coach Bobby Johnson said, "we were going to Earl if they covered a certain way."

In other words: if the Vols were brave enough (dumb enough?) to use man coverage on Bennett with Jason Allen long out of the lineup, the Commodores would be throwing to him every time. The sound of 106,000 fans groaning turned into intermittent shrieks, almost like the ones you hear in a bad horror movie, when Bennett beat Johnson again and hauled in a 31-yard pass down the right sideline. The secret was out.

"I was going to Earl," Cutler said later. "We knew it, and they knew it."

But did they? The Vols didn't make any adjustments. On the next play, Inky Johnson—now completely overwhelmed by Bennett and the magnitude of the moment—interfered with Bennett on another pass down the right sideline to give Vanderbilt first-and-goal at the 5.

"They were in man coverage," Bennett said later. "Cover 1. They didn't change anything."

Not even on a history-changing play. On first down, Cutler called for a double slant in the end zone. The Vols didn't triple-team Bennett. They didn't double-team Bennett. They didn't play zone or really change their defensive look at all. Bennett started his route to the left, then cut inside of Johnson toward the right. Safety Jonathan Hefney was a moment late getting to the ball, and Cutler threw a perfect strike to Bennett in the end zone with 1:11 left. Touchdown. It took 29 seconds.

There were still a few lingering shrieks. No one booed. The Vanderbilt cheering section was too small, too insignificant in the sea of orange to create much ruckus. History, for Tennessee, was ending swiftly, silently and calmly, except on the Commodores' sideline.

Cutler, and who could blame him, admittedly thought his team would pull a Vanderbilt. "We scored too early," he mumbled to Johnson when he got to the sideline.

Not, "Did you see that pass!" Not, "Oh my gosh, we're beating Tennessee!" Not, "We just scored the game-winning touchdown and made history!"

We scored too early.

And Vanderbilt went right to work being Vanderbilt, committing a 15-yard roughing-the-passer penalty on Tennessee's first play from scrimmage. On the next play, the Commodores allowed slow-footed and gimpy Rick Clausen to somehow scramble for 13 yards to give Tennessee first-and-10 at the Vanderbilt 46 with a minute to play. On second down, Clausen hit a wide-open Jayson Swain for 31 yards to the Vanderbilt 17. Maybe Cutler was right.

And then a strange phenomenon, one not seen in twenty-two years, suddenly transpired under a gray sky at Neyland Stadium.

Tennessee pulled a Vanderbilt.

Yet it looked so much like Tennessee.

Following a six-yard scramble by Clausen, officials penalized the Vols five yards for spiking the ball too fast. On the next play, Clausen overthrew open tight end Chris Brown in the end zone. On third down, Clausen's pass bounced off the fingertips of receiver Bret Smith in the back of the end zone.

Fourth down, one second left. Clausen rolls left as the horn sounds, the only noise audible inside an anxious Neyland Stadium. No one is open. None of Tennessee's receivers—hailed as some of the nation's best before the season—could get free against the Vanderbilt secondary. Clausen is running out of room. He heaves a desperation pass toward the end zone as he absorbs a hit, and Vanderbilt freshman Jared Fagan picks it off at the goal line. He runs three yards and falls down.

Silence.

Vanderbilt players charged toward the small cheering section, some of them crying.

"We beat Tennessee," Bennett said, "and that's something that hasn't happened in like a hundred years or something."

Same old Vandy? Not this time. Big bad Tennessee? Hardly.

Ranked No. 3 in the pre-season and expected to play for a national title at the Rose Bowl, the only roses the Vols would see were the ones covering their grave. The season was over. Next weekend's game at Kentucky was meaningless. So was the trip to Knoxville by representatives from the Music City and Independence bowls. The Vols, 4–6 and 2–5 in the SEC, would not be playing in a bowl game this year for the first time since 1988.

"I had to bite myself in the locker room to make sure this was real," said linebacker Jason Mitchell, who sacrificed his career to play his final home game and lose to Vanderbilt. This wasn't quite the grand finale he had imagined.

The finale inside Neyland Stadium also included some other unimaginable events. Several disgusted Tennessee players, including Richie Gandy and Rick Clausen, left their helmets in the end zone for the managers to pick up. Right tackle Albert Toeaina, the six-foot-six, 350-pound combustible junior college transfer from California, scared an already shaken Tennessee crowd near the end zone by slinging his helmet against the padded wall that surrounds the field. The booming sound startled everyone within earshot.

As if losing to Vanderbilt wasn't frightening enough, Tennessee fans were now dodging helmets.

Toeaina's rampage was far from over. His senior day would certainly be memorable. According to Scott Liston, a Jumbotron cameraman who positioned himself underneath the goalpost,

Toeaina spat on him as he left the field. Rob Lewis, the humorous writer for volquest.com, said he witnessed a fuming Toeaina curse out Liston and spit in his direction. The media explained the incident to Fulmer, who called Lewis's cell phone later in the evening and said Toeaina's "butt would be on the bench" if the allegations were true. Lewis said Fulmer sounded like a beaten man.

Fulmer also had to explain why so many Tennessee helmets remained in the end zone following the game. The action was viewed as a sign of disrespect to the university.

"I would say they're immature and don't really appreciate what Tennessee has to offer," said defensive tackle Jesse Mahelona, one of just three Tennessee players to show up for post-game interviews.

Everyone in the Tennessee program grew so upset over the season and, in particular, the loss to Vanderbilt that they didn't stop to consider how ridiculous the reaction was to the helmet incident. There was the *Seinfeld*-like humor of the increasingly bizarre Toeaina episode, humor that wasn't appreciated by anyone wearing orange. Instead of searching for an offensive coordinator or studying game film, Fulmer spent the Monday following the loss studying film from *after* the game to determine who had left their helmets on the field. He examined his own film and footage taken from local television stations, determined Gandy had left his helmet on the field and suspended him for the first half of the Kentucky game.

Whatever.

Based on Liston's allegations, Fulmer suspended Toeaina for one game, effectively ending the senior's career at Tennessee. But Toeaina's father, Alex, produced video footage—think the Zapruder film of *JFK* and *Seinfeld* fame—of Toeaina leaving the field. The film shows Toeaina spitting toward Liston's feet, not at his face. Liston's head moves down, and to the right, dodging the spit aimed his way.

"I didn't quite get the part where he threw his helmet because my battery was low," Alex Toeaina told a TV station. "But when he threw his helmet, that's when I fired up the camera again, and then I videoed that. I didn't notice anything happen until Sunday night when he was suspended and allegedly spat at the cameraman's face.

"My footage shows the back of his head. You can't see the facial expression. The cameraman said that Albert said some word to him. I asked Albert if he said it, and he said, 'Yes I did, Dad.' He apologized for that. He doesn't apologize for spitting at the man's face. He spat, but he didn't spit at his face. I don't think Albert's the kind of kid that would do that. I can't see it."

Liston said Toeaina spit on his face and even showed witnesses the saliva on his camera. Was there a second spitter? Did Toeaina's spit take a sharp left turn just before it hit the ground?

That's one magic loogie.

This was what had become of Tennessee football.

"I guess sometimes before you start building back everything, you've got to hit rock bottom," Fulmer said. "This is about rock bottom."

Charlie Brown kicked the football. The band geek took the prettiest girl in school to the prom. A pair beat a royal flush. Wile E. Coyote caught the Road Runner.

Vanderbilt beat Tennessee.

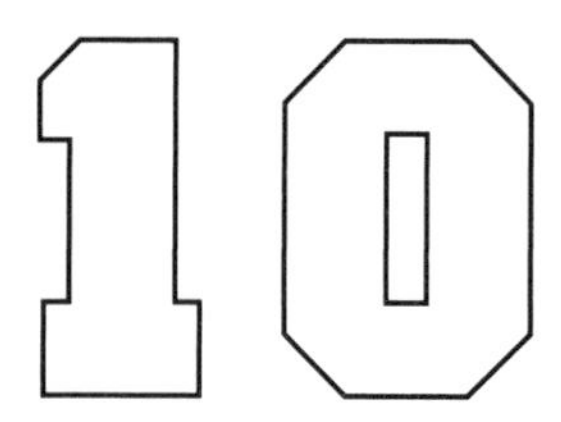

The Aftermath

FOLLOWING THE STAGGERING loss to Vanderbilt, Tennessee rebounded with a 27–8 win at Kentucky.

No one cared.

Tennessee fans, however, did care about the phone call Phillip Fulmer made to offensive line coach Jimmy Ray Stephens after the game. Fulmer had promised much-anticipated changes at the end of the season. The sound of the horn and three zeroes on the clock at Commonwealth Stadium said it: the 2005 football season was officially over. Stephens' cell phone ring signaled the beginning of a new season. Coach-hunting season.

"When you get back to Knoxville," Fulmer told Stephens, "stop by and give me a holler."

Gulp. Stephens, a bright, approachable fifty-one-year-old who worked at Tennessee for four seasons following a stint under Steve Spurrier at Florida, knew Fulmer wasn't organizing a fishing trip or planning to ask Stephens about his family. Stephens knew he was gone. He just didn't understand why. In Stephens' estimation, only nine of the nineteen sacks Tennessee allowed—the second fewest in the conference behind Auburn—were the fault of Tennessee's offensive linemen. The Vols had also improved their rushing totals, albeit against worse teams, once Fulmer finally decided halfway through the season he wanted to establish the run. The Vols finished 79th nationally in rushing.

And then Stephens said he remembered a reporter's question early in his tenure at Tennessee: which is tougher, coaching offensive linemen under Steve Spurrier and protecting his precious quarterbacks, or coaching offensive linemen under a former lineman in Phillip Fulmer? Stephens didn't yet know the answer.

He did on Saturday night, November 26, at about 8 p.m., following a five-minute meeting with Fulmer. Stephens didn't even ask the head coach why he had been fired.

"The thing that's so shocking was I felt the offensive line was the most consistent part of the offense the whole season," Stephens told the *Knoxville News-Sentinel.* "Apparently, some big-time donor had written his opinion of some changes that needed to be made, and mine and Pat Washington's name were in that. But I thought that wouldn't happen, because Coach Fulmer had nothing but positive praise for me in the past.

"I think in his heart, Coach Fulmer knows I did a good job.

I've got to believe he's got pressure from the outside to make this decision."

Stephens was partially right. Fulmer didn't make the decision by himself. Tennessee's new offensive coordinator helped.

David Cutcliffe was back.

And when Stephens left Fulmer's office after a short meeting, he walked right past wide receivers coach Pat Washington. Fulmer then fired Washington, the former Auburn quarterback who'd spent eleven years on the Tennessee staff and received the brunt of criticism during the 5–6 season. His receivers caught just eleven touchdown passes a year after hauling in twenty-seven.

Sophomore Robert Meachem, whom Fulmer had called the most advanced freshman receiver he had ever coached and a sure bet to leave school early for the NFL, *led* the Vols with 34.8 yards receiving per game and caught a grand total of two touchdowns. The NFL would survive without him. Junior Jayson Swain, one of the most highly recruited receivers in the South, scored the same number of touchdowns as his embattled receivers coach in 2005. None. An aggressive reporter called Swain at his Huntsville, Ala., home after the 2005 season to ask if he was staying at Tennessee for his senior year. Swain cracked up laughing.

"With the season I had?" he said, still chuckling.

The fired Washington didn't return phone calls or release a statement. He disappeared, just like the potential of his receivers. The fallout from Tennessee's worst season in sixteen years had begun.

"I appreciate everything Jimmy Ray and Pat have done for Tennessee over the years," Fulmer said. "This was a difficult decision to make, but I feel it is in the best interest of the future of our football program."

And with that last ridiculous comment, the fallout on Tennessee's offensive staff ended.

Difficult decision? The decision was so hard on Fulmer it took him all of four hours and a conversation with Cutcliffe to cut Stephens and Washington loose from the program. Stephens landed a job three hours away at Middle Tennessee State and Washington ended up at Kansas State.

The season was over, but the ramifications of finishing 5–6 were far from complete. The Vols endured one more departure, only this one was unexpected. Offensive lineman Rob Smith, a media day staple who grew noticeably weary of the questions about Tennessee's wretched offense, elected to skip his senior season and turn pro despite learning he would likely be a fourth-round draft pick. (Smith would not be selected.) Smith was a fierce, tough competitor who started twenty-four straight games—extremely rare for a guard/center—and played hurt without ever complaining. But not even Smith could muster the desire to hang around the program any longer. The Stephens firing upset him, and all the losses wounded even the toughest player on the team.

"I know a lot of people won't agree with this and will tell me that I'm making the wrong decision," Smith said. "But this is what I wanted. If I can't be 110 percent motivated to do something, then I'm cheating everybody. And I wouldn't have been 110 percent motivated if I had come back to Tennessee next season."

Fulmer, on the other hand, would be back next season

holding a rare document—a contract without increased pay or bonuses. It's also rare for athletic director Mike Hamilton not to be giving away money after the season. He'd given former basketball coach Buzz Peterson a huge raise for making the NIT in 2003, and later regretted it. He made Fulmer one of the three highest-paid college football coaches in the country at $2.05 million per season after the Vols played in a non-BCS bowl game for the sixth straight year in 2004. Imagine if Peterson had made the NCAA Tournament and Fulmer had actually gotten Tennessee in the Sugar Bowl. Hamilton might have offered them his house.

But for the first time in his career, Fulmer did not get a raise or contract extension in 2005.

"I view raises and extensions as a reward for meeting and or exceeding expectations," Hamilton said, "and we didn't do that this year."

Said Fulmer, "I didn't expect a raise, and I didn't deserve one with the way things went this season."

No kidding. But Fulmer seemed genuinely embarrassed by the 5–6 season and even sent the following e-mail to 38,000 season ticket holders:

> Dear Tennessee Fans,
>
> I wanted to take a moment to thank you for the great support you give our team. Your passion and pride for our program is what makes us special!

This year was a disappointing season for everyone in the Tennessee family. We started this season with great expectations and failed to live up to those expectations. I assure you that no one is happy about our season—especially me, and I know that our fans deserve better than what we produced this year.

Now that the season is over, I am taking a step back and re-evaluating the entire program. We're doing a lot of things well—especially our defense, but obviously not enough. We grossly underachieved offensively, and special teams were erratic at best. As I've said before, the results this year are unacceptable and accountability starts with me.

My staff and I have great determination to get things back on track. In order to get things turned around, we first have to look at what happened this season. I'm doing a complete audit of everything in our program. No stone will be left unturned and no question left unanswered as to what went wrong.

I've taken some steps already, and others are in short order. I have made some coaching changes to move forward. I feel the addition of David Cutcliffe as offensive coordinator is a great step forward for us. He is a great football coach, but better yet he's a leader and teacher. He will challenge our thinking, be creative with our offense and very demanding of our players.

> I appreciate the support and patience I've received from the administration and Tennessee fans everywhere to make the adjustments I need to make to get back to where I believe we should be. We have had many great moments, games and seasons together and will again. Tennessee football is about pride, and it's my first priority to restore that pride.
>
> Go Vols!
>
> *Phillip Fulmer*

Now writing an e-mail is a nice gesture. But no Tennessee fan felt better about the season or the future because Fulmer's heartfelt apology appeared in their in-box. Besides, the e-mail wasn't necessary. Fulmer had already given Tennessee fans a reason to believe in him.

David Cutcliffe was back. Fulmer hired him twenty-four hours after the Kentucky game and introduced him the following day at a Monday evening press conference. Fulmer, often called too loyal to his assistants, needed only two days to rearrange his offensive coaching staff. Only running backs coach Trooper Taylor and tight ends coach/recruiting coordinator Greg Adkins survived, and sentiments quickly improved toward the Tennessee program. Sure, Smith was leaving a year early, and Tennessee was stumbling on the recruiting trail, but Washington was gone, and Cutcliffe was back.

Cutcliffe had actually come back months before Sanders'

offense turned into the Bad News Vols. Temporarily out of coaching after leaving Notre Dame on June 1, 2005, due to the effects of triple bypass heart surgery in March, Cutcliffe elected to recover in Knoxville—where he and his wife, Karen, had spent most of their married life—and appeared on local radio shows throughout the fall. He even took in one of Tennessee's fall practices in August.

"He recognized a lot of the calls," Fulmer said at the time, laughing. "That's a little disconcerting."

He did not recognize the results. Discipline and structure had once defined Cutcliffe's practices on Haslam Field. Dishevelment and laziness had defined Tennessee's practices on offense during the fall. He couldn't comment on it too much back then.

He could now.

"With David," Archie Manning said, "they've got someone with six years of head coaching experience that isn't afraid to tell Phillip what he thinks."

And here's what Cutcliffe thought: Tennessee's practice habits stunk. Cutcliffe met with the offense just before his introduction to the media and offered a simple, yet powerful message: Do it my way or get the hell out.

Cutcliffe isn't a fiery guy. He won't rip his shirt off like men's basketball coach Bruce Pearl or sling chairs at a chalkboard. He has the sterile, polite personality of Fulmer around the media, and it's easy to see why the two are such good friends. But, admittedly, he's one stubborn football coach.

"And I'm still hard-headed," Cutcliffe said. "I'm probably

more intense about attention to detail as I get older because I understand the importance of it even more. I guess they say all of us lose a little patience as we get a little older. I hope we can all make it fun, but they're going to do it the way we want them to do it. It's as simple as that."

Determining Cutcliffe's success in developing quarterbacks is both difficult and quite simple to figure out. At Tennessee, Cutcliffe groomed NFL star Peyton Manning and then coached his brother, current N.Y. Giants quarterback Eli Manning, at Ole Miss. Two quarterbacks, two No. 1 picks. Not bad.

But consider the pedigree of both quarterbacks, their incredible raw talent, the teachings of their father and former NFL star, Archie Manning, along with their tireless work ethic, and no wonder the critics said a trained monkey—hell, an *untrained* monkey—could develop the Manning brothers into NFL starters. No other Cutcliffe-coached quarterback had accomplished much at the next level.

And if many people did indeed doubt Cutcliffe, he would get a chance to prove himself during his second stint at Tennessee. As a true freshman, quarterback Erik Ainge was brilliant, completing 55.1 percent of his passes for 1,452 yards, seventeen touchdowns and nine interceptions. He won games against Georgia, Florida and Alabama. But he was atrocious as a sophomore in Fulmer's pick-a-name-out-of-the-hat quarterback rotation, completing forty-six percent of his passes for 737 yards, five touchdowns and seven interceptions. His mechanics looked terrible at times, he threw ill-advised passes into coverage, rarely dumped off easy completions to his backs, made stupefying decisions like the bridal bouquet toss at LSU, and racked up intentional grounding penalties instead of taking sacks. In short, Ainge made all the mistakes Manning quarterbacks did not.

"Erik never got in any kind of rhythm; he never got comfortable," said Cutcliffe, who watched tape of every 2005 game after taking the job. "He was either in a hurry, or ended up out of balance throwing the ball. He would throw a good ball on occasion, but he never had a consistent throwing motion. So we're going to start from scratch and see what happens. Erik has a lot of talent. He has plenty of arm strength, and his feet are good enough."

Fulmer, whose staff was working lengthy hours on the recruiting trail with two assistants gone, hoped Cutcliffe could also help in recruiting. Here was an assistant who had not only earned acclaim developing quarterbacks but also led UT offenses to the top of the SEC in rushing three times. He had even worked for a few months under Notre Dame coach Charlie Weis. Surely the nation's top offensive players would flock to Knoxville.

Only they didn't. Tennessee started the season strong in recruiting, landing Alabama prep tight end Michael Goggans and scratching back into the race with Florida State for defensive end/tight end Brandon Warren, who lived fifteen miles from campus and was considered the state's top prospect. Then 5–6 happened, and suddenly the nation's top recruits had other plans. Prep stars had tests and basketball games and family business on the weekends they were scheduled to visit Tennessee. The Vols were like a wart-covered blind date. The wart was a 5–6 record.

Calls weren't getting returned, excuses were being made and, finally, even the players who had been committed to Tennessee started seeing other people.

Fulmer is considered one of nation's best recruiters. But the 2005 season would challenge his philosophy of recruiting more than any other. Fulmer recruits nationally, and convincing athletes who live 2,500 miles away to play for a 5–6 team would prove to be the most difficult recruiting task of his career. As Tennessee skidded into the Alabama game, linebacker and California native Kevin Simon said players didn't move across the country—leaving family, friends and high school teammates behind—to play for a losing team.

The Vols were a losing team. Heading into the first big recruiting weekend following the season, the Vols had ten commitments for the 2006 class. Two, Daniel Lincoln and Lones Seiber, were kickers. They planned to join senior field goal kicker James Wilhoit and sophomore punter Britton Colquitt on the team in 2006, giving the Vols one of the top soccer teams on campus. Three other commitments were tight ends, which meant half of Tennessee's commitments were either kickers or tight ends. And since tight ends usually serve on special teams, Tennessee's extra-point unit would be quite formidable in about three years. The Vols recovered a little and picked up some commitments in January, then stumbled toward signing day like a drunk.

Three highly touted offensive linemen picked other schools over Tennessee. Warren picked Florida State, meaning Fulmer failed to land the state's top prospect for the second straight year.

(The Vols lost receiver Patrick Turner to Southern Cal in 2005.) Kelvin Sheppard and Perry Riley—two highly-recruited high school teammates in Georgia—picked LSU, then leaned toward Tennessee, then signed with LSU at the last moment. Virginia safety Greg Davis picked West Virginia over Tennessee. North Carolina defensive lineman Aleric Mullins chose the Tar Heels. Even one of the kickers decommitted.

Then came the big blow. Goggans, who one day earlier had confirmed his commitment to Tennessee, stunned Fulmer by signing with Auburn. A room full of Tennessee coaches had kept him on speaker phone for two hours the night before, pleading with him to stick to the commitment.

"I think I made the right decision," Goggans said. "Auburn won my heart."

Fulmer, notorious for landing late commitments to fill out a class, went 0-for-signing-day and finished with the nation's No. 23 class as one of college football's great recruiting closers blew several saves. It was the worst signing class of Fulmer's career. Out of frustration, he blasted the recruiting rankings and, without naming names, ripped the players who'd backed out of their commitments to Tennessee.

"We had some kids lie to us," Fulmer said. "Flat lie to us. There's a few, not everybody, who make it a show. They have no respect, not only for their parents, but for the schools who are spending time and money and effort. You might be coming, you might not. But just be honest. That's the biggest thing.

"I saw more kids this year go against the wishes of their parents.

Regardless if you're eighteen years old, it's amazing. It's really amazing. I don't call it all disrespect, but it's certainly not what you're used to."

Those comments absolutely bewildered Tennessee's recruiting writers. Fulmer protested the recruiting rankings, yet he hadn't said a word when Tennessee hauled in the nation's top class the previous year. Fulmer whined about decommitments, but he typically closes well because he steals recruits from other schools. Heck, Sheppard and Riley were both LSU commitments when Fulmer attempted to make his late push. Fulmer complained about players going against the wishes of their parents, but several players on Tennessee's team had come far from home to play for Fulmer. Kevin Simon's father, for instance, was incensed when his son signed with Tennessee.

All a bunch of hypocritical whining.

"They can change their perception by getting back to a BCS game," Scout.com's Scott Kennedy said, "but this recruiting class is not going to do that for them next year."

Ouch.

"You get sad. You get mad. You get flustered," Fulmer said.

And with that, the fallout of the 2005 season was finally over.

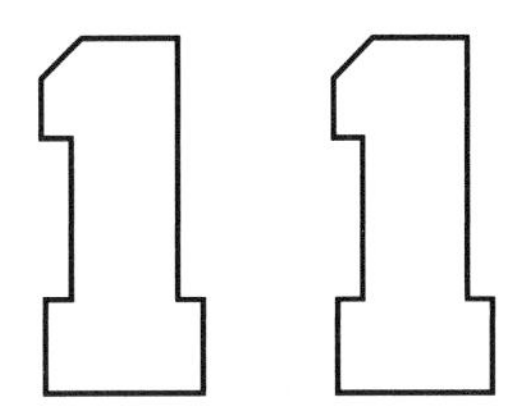

What Happened?

In August of 2005, Randy Sanders was considered a master with quarterbacks and one of the most valuable assistants in the SEC. By November, he was fishing for bass instead of the next great recruit.

In August, Phillip Fulmer was a beloved coach with a new, lavish contract who took an unheralded team of underclassmen to the SEC title game and then swiped almost every high school stud in the South. By November, he couldn't get through his weekly coaches' radio show without an irate caller berating him on the air and couldn't get through a week without watching a recruit commit elsewhere. "Fulmer's house," the orange port-a-potty had read following the Georgia game.

In August, Tennessee fans were gobbling up every pre-season magazine, cramming message boards with excited chatter and counting down the days, hours, minutes and seconds until the 2005 season. By November, they were counting down the days, hours, minutes and seconds until the 2005 season was over.

In August, Tennessee was the sexy pick to win the national championship, a team loaded with savvy, talented veterans and all-conference stars. By November, the Vols were losing to Vanderbilt, allegedly spitting on cameramen and trying to avoid a last-place finish in the SEC East.

Three months is half a major league baseball season, one-third of a NASCAR season, the average length of an internship and all the time needed to transform a proud college football program into a laughingstock shunned by most of the nation's top prospects.

"If we don't go to the Rose Bowl," defensive tackle Jesse Mahelona had said in August, "then we did something wrong."

Did they ever. But what? How could so many analysts, coaches, assistants, players and media members be so wrong about Tennessee?

What happened?

And then you think back to the beginning, to the first lightning strike before the actual lightning strike, when a grainy video appeared on the websites of Tennessee's newspapers and TV stations the day before players reported to fall practice.

Tony McDaniel wasn't considered one of the troubled players on Tennessee's football team. Before his video-taped knockout blow of a fellow student in January, McDaniel's name hadn't appeared on any police reports or in court appearance records in Knoxville. He was reserved during interviews and on the practice field, where Fulmer once said McDaniel "looks like Tarzan and plays like Jane."

But Fulmer's mere two-game suspension of McDaniel, who broke four bones in Edward Goodrich's face, stunned those who watched the recording of the vicious cheap shot and the subsequent disturbing reaction, and it sent a message that was apparently ingrained in the minds of the Tennessee players in 2005: we'll protect you. You can hit, steal, wrestle, fight, break bones, knock out teeth and send people to the hospital. Just help us win a national championship.

We'll protect you.

The evidence was on the practice field. Mistakes went unpunished, uncorrected and, evidently, unresolved.

"We had no discipline," tight end Chris Brown said. "That was the biggest problem."

Said Fulmer, "Hindsight is 20-20, but you look back and say, 'Was our tempo good enough? Were our demands and discipline good enough? Were we taking from meeting rooms to the individual periods to group periods to team work the right message? We were doing the right things, and we were doing it at a tempo that allowed us to be effective? Looking back and with our offensive struggles, there was something missing somewhere. Now, was it attitude? Was it discipline? Was it too much? Were we giving them too much information? It doesn't matter what we know. It's what they know how to execute.

"I don't think everything is broken. But certainly from an offensive standpoint, there needs to be more accountability and more responsiveness. We tried to ratchet it up at different times all year long. It's almost like putting your finger in the dyke holes. There's one hole here and one hole there."

Here's another hole: receivers and offensive linemen gained weight without repercussions. Jayson Swain was noticeably bigger as the season wore on, but the offensive linemen would eat the weight he gained for breakfast each day. The Vols' offensive line averaged 334 pounds against UAB and got fatter as the season wore on. Former UT linemen Bubba Miller criticized Tennessee's offensive line for being too soft and slow, and another former lineman, who didn't want to be named, said he giggled when he watched Tennessee's offensive guards pull on a running play or screens. After the season, even Fulmer said the blocking on Tennessee's screen passes was "terrible."

Much later in 2005, at a Tennessee basketball game, a defensive player said, "You know what's crazy? Think back to the first scrimmage. The offense threw it all over us. Meachem was beating Jason Allen for touchdowns on deep plays. We couldn't stop them."

The Vols got worse in a hurry. Receivers dropped passes, linemen missed assignments, and the quarterbacks, particularly Erik Ainge, threw the ball all over the place without much admonishment at all. The prevailing attitude seemed to be this: get it right the next time, we're still talented; it'll be okay, we're Tennessee.

"The biggest lesson I learned is there are no shortcuts," Ainge said. "I think we, as a team, thought we were pretty good early. All the hype we got, I think we might have let it get to us a little bit."

It was an attitude Fulmer helped ingrain in the team during the pre-season, when he was talking about the Rose Bowl and making comparisons between Ainge and Peyton Manning. He added pressure and a touch of undeserved arrogance. "I was much, much too optimistic in the pre-season about our football team and probably added pressures to our team," Fulmer admitted. "You'll never hear that again. I learned a great lesson because I'm usually very cautious and optimistic. I don't know if I added pressure to them or allowed them to think they were better than they were. This season has reflected very much some of the assumptions that were made like, 'Hey, we're going to have a good football team.'"

Texas Tech basketball coach Bobby Knight infamously kicks players out of practice for failing to give good effort. It also happened at Tennessee. One player, offensive lineman Albert Toeaina, did leave practice out of frustration after throwing his helmet. Fulmer sent a manager to go find him. They let him back in, and he started the next game.

We'll protect you.

"It was more of a thing that when we messed up in practice early on, we were thinking, 'Oh well, we'll recover from it because we're too good of a team not to,'" center Richie Gandy said. The evidence was in the police blotter. Of all the Tennessee players arrested for fighting, Fulmer never handed out a punishment longer than three games. Penalties for rearranging a frat boy's face never increased as the line for football player mug shots lengthened at the Knoxville Police Department. Brawls at the University Center, nightclubs, dorms and basketball courts disrupted team chemistry. The Vols took a beating in the national media, which pegged them as thugs. Well-behaved players eyed the troublemakers.

"There were times in my mind I was thinking, 'We've got some more problems than what's on the surface,'" left guard Rob Smith said. But Fulmer had set one standard, no exceptions: send a kid to the hospital, take two games off.

"I'm not pointing a finger to go back to last April and think that caused our problems in September. I don't think that," Fulmer said. "But if I had managed ourselves a little bit better and corrected some things on the front end, I don't know how many games we would have won, but we would have been a better football team."

We'll protect you.

The evidence was in Jason Allen's home. Allen, who had led the SEC in tackles playing safety as a junior, demanded to play cornerback in 2005 during a meeting with Fulmer and John Chavis, or he was entering the NFL draft. Allen acted as though he was returning solely to accomplish personal goals and help the team win a championship, but everyone knew he also wanted to boost his draft stock—the NFL predicted he was a second-round pick—by playing corner. If he was coming back, he was playing corner. Never mind that, in 2004, the Vols rotated safeties more than they did quarterbacks in the 2005 season without ever finding a competent starter. Never mind that the move forced Tennessee to use diminutive cornerback Jonathan Hefney at safety.

Fulmer welcomed Allen back to Knoxville, put him at corner and everyone at Allen's press conference smiled and patted each other on the back.

We'll protect you.

The evidence was in the quarterback rotation. Rick Clausen beat Erik Ainge in every statistical category during fall camp except for one: the amount of potential Fulmer saw in Ainge. If Fulmer had named Ainge the starting quarterback based on potential as he'd said, there was no reason to hold a competition. Instead, he struggled to look Clausen in the eye and tell the senior his career was pretty much finished aside from carrying the occasional clipboard.

So he didn't. Fulmer never committed to a starter and never hurt anyone's feelings, and his indecisiveness created a controversy unlike anyone had ever seen in Knoxville. The quarterback rotation shredded the fabric of the team and Ainge's confidence. It broke the rhythm of the receivers and forced everyone to pick sides. Following the season, a reporter interrupted C.J. Fayton's discussion of Clausen's calming influence in the huddle and asked if Ainge brought the same calming influence to the huddle.

"No comment," he said.

The rotation of starters went as follows: Ainge, Clausen, Ainge, Clausen, Clausen, Clausen, Clausen, Ainge, Ainge, Clausen, Ainge. Not counting his demotions between games, Fulmer benched Ainge eight times. The kid's mind was a wreck.

"Was it a distraction?" Fulmer asked after the season. "Probably."

But, hey, at least Clausen got to play against UAB after Ainge had led Tennessee on two straight scoring drives to open the season.

We'll protect you.

The attitude continued like this until each Saturday, when no one could protect the Vols from their opponents. No one could step in and save them. An overachieving Georgia squad and the grief-stricken LSU Tigers, two teams that figured they should beat up on the other team instead of fellow students or each other, played for the SEC championship. Tennessee's season was already over when Georgia hoisted the SEC trophy. For the seventh straight year, Tennessee was not part of the ceremony. "The school up in Knoxville folded when they went through some hard times," Florida coach Urban Meyer told a gathering of Gator fans in Daytona Beach, Fla.

Which brings us to the bigger, possibly more accurate picture of the program, one Tennessee fans are hesitant to acknowledge and Fulmer will never embrace: perhaps the big, bad Vols of the 1990s simply aren't that good anymore. A comparison of Fulmer's first ten seasons to his last four is startling.

Overall record

1992–2001: 95–20

2002–2005: 33–17

Top-ten finishes
1992–2001: 6
2002–2005: 0

NFL first-round draft choices
1992–2001: 11
2002–2005: 1

Losses of thirteen points or more
1992–2001: 5
2002–2005: 9

Losses of seventeen points or more at Neyland Stadium
1992–2001: 1
2002–2005: 5

Record versus top twenty-five teams
1992–2001: 30-16-1
2002-2005: 6-12

On Tennessee's annual fundraising tour following the season, officials tried to put a spin their struggles by emphasizing that the Vols had won more games than any other SEC program over the last ten years. That was true. But it was also not the entire story. In the last four, the Vols were fourth behind Georgia, LSU and Auburn (and just one game ahead of Florida during the disastrous Ron Zook Era). Maybe the offense is antiquated, the talent level is down, player development is weak and Tennessee is lucky a season like 2005 didn't happen much sooner or more often. Maybe we all should have seen this coming. Entering the 2005 season, there were red flags, blinking lights, billowing smoke, detour signs, caution tape—and the Tennessee football program just kept strutting on through until it fell off the cliff and, in Fulmer's words, "hit rock bottom."

From 1998 to 2002, NFL commissioner Paul Tagliabue called the names of nine first-round draft picks from Tennessee. Only one since—Jason Allen in the 2006 draft to the Miami Dolphins. The only time Tagliabue uttered the word *Tennessee* during the first round of the draft from 2003 to '05 was announcing the pick of the Tennessee Titans. In 2003, the Vols' highest pick was linebacker Eddie Moore late in the second round. The following year, the NFL Draft's first *day* went by without a single Tennessee player taken. Finally, late on Sunday afternoon when even Mel Kiper Jr. was running out of players that he knew, the New York Giants picked Gibril Wilson in the fifth round. Quarterback Casey Clausen, who started for four seasons, wasn't even picked (LSU's Matt Mauck, who wanted to be a dentist, and Wyoming's Casey Bramlet both got selected). And in 2005, only three Vols were drafted. And one of those picks was a punter, Dustin Colquitt.

But ask the recruiting gurus, and they'll tell you Tennessee's talent level is just fine. In 1996, the Vols ranked third nationally in recruiting by Rivals.com. The following year, they were fifth. In 1998, they were seventh; in 2000, they ranked second, then earned another No. 2 ranking in 2002. Recruiting rankings aren't an exact science—Pittsburgh Steelers star Ben Roethlisberger was considered the 50th-best quarterback in the 2000 class—but such a long trend of hauling in the nation's top players typically translates into lots of wins and happy fans.

Tennessee's fans are not happy. Developing players is a problem. Yeah, a major issue is coaching. "And there's your reason for Tennessee not having success," noted NFL draft analyst Mike Detillier said. "They aren't developing players, particularly on offense, at Tennessee like you used to see. Those players aren't getting much better. And it boils down to coaching."

Fast-forward four years from Tennessee's highly-regarded 2002 class to the 2006 NFL draft. That class produced the same number of draft picks on the offensive side of the ball as the Tennessee School of Beauty in Knoxville—zero. To find a Tennessee offensive player picked higher than the sixth round, you have to go back to the 2003 draft. Fulmer pleaded with high school offensive stars like Casey Clausen, Jason Respert, Sean Young, Jabari Davis, C.J. Fayton, Derrick Tinsley and Gerald Riggs Jr. to give Tennessee a chance. After their four years, those players, all undrafted, were pleading with the NFL to give them a chance. And here's another interesting recent trend concerning Tennessee and the NFL and possibly the most indicting knock on the program.

The Vols are still filling out NFL rosters, hearing their names called on Sundays and having their smiling faces shown on Monday night football telecasts. Defensive backs Rashad Baker and

Jabari Greer went undrafted in 2004, then started in the same secondary in Buffalo one year later. Wilson is one of the Giants' best defensive players. The Dallas Cowboys took tight end Jason Witten in the third round in 2003. One year later, Witten was playing in the Pro Bowl. Troy Fleming was an under-used fullback/running back who rarely cracked the starting lineup at Tennessee until 2004, when he was playing for the Titans.

These players starred in high school, played at Tennessee, tumbled in the draft and starred once again in the NFL, as if playing at Tennessee was a detriment to a player's draft status. Maybe the NFL was overlooking Tennessee's players. Or maybe the problem was in Knoxville. "I find it hard to believe all those kids that every school in the country wanted just didn't pan out," Detillier said.

This is not to say the Vols are the SEC's new Vanderbilt. But they certainly aren't the old Tennessee. When I joined the beat in 2002, the Vols were just four years removed from a national championship. They nearly contended for one in 1999 and were a fourth-quarter-meltdown against LSU away from playing for the title in 2001. In four years, I covered the following bowls: Peach, Peach, Cotton, no bowl. Not exactly a murderer's row of post-season games, but a slate many schools in the nation would plaster across the covers of media guides. And the Vols did post two straight ten-win seasons in 2003 and 2004.

"We've had a target on us because we had that success," Fulmer said. "We competed for the championship in '01 and in '04. A lot of things depend on injuries, scheduling and who stays healthy.

People really don't want to listen to this, but the 85 scholarship limit makes it to where everyone has a chance to be good. If you lose a couple of guys, or somebody's not coming through for you, it makes a difference."

But it's the way Tennessee played during those seasons that was overlooked. The Vols finished 10–3 in 2003, but got blown out three times (the 28–21 loss at Auburn does not nearly indicate how much Tennessee got outplayed). In 2004, Tennessee beat Florida by two points (thanks to the botched clock management by the officials, which earned them a suspension), Georgia by five, Ole Miss by four, Alabama by four, Vanderbilt by five and Kentucky by six. Six games won by six points or less, a record in the SEC. Everyone lauded Fulmer's ability to coach in close games, raved about how Tennessee thrived in pressure situations and heaped praise upon the conditioning staff without considering a frightening thought: a missed field goal here or an unlucky bounce there, and the Vols were a five-win team. Only no one gave much credence to the idea, because Tennessee winning just five games under Fulmer was a ridiculous notion.

That is, until a missed field goal here and an unlucky bounce there *did* happen, and the Vols *were* a five-win team. Perhaps we all should have seen it coming, especially considering Tennessee's schedule in 2005: at Florida, at LSU, at Georgia, at Alabama and at Notre Dame. If the Vols' luck ran out, the season would turn ugly.

It was real ugly.

"We've played really hard in the football games, and it's been very unusual, some of the things that have cost us games, and that adds to the frustration," Fulmer said. "If you just said, 'Well, they're a lot better than us, we got our cans kicked,' that's one thing, but that hasn't been the case this season. It's been a lot of our own doing and some injuries. It's just really been frustrating. If we just play a little better and disregard injuries and disregard the tough schedule, we're not in the predicament we're in right now."

Fulmer scoffed at the idea that Tennessee's decline was a trend and not a simple abberation. The injuries to players like Gerald Riggs Jr. and Jason Allen, the treacherous schedule and the unlucky bounces on fumbles created what Fulmer frequently called a "perfect storm" for a 5–6 season.

That first scrimmage sure did start with a lightning strike.

12

The Future

PHILLIP FULMER SLUNG a water bottle against a wall in anger and screamed at his players.

One year after a flurry of arrests made Tennessee a national punch line and served as a prelude to a 5–6 season, two defensive players found themselves in trouble just weeks after the conclusion of spring practice. Fulmer hurriedly called a team meeting and blasted his players. According to a police report, fifth-year senior Marvin Mitchell threatened to "knock out" a customer at a gas station during the early morning hours of Monday, May 1. He reeked of alcohol and was uncooperative with authorities, telling one police officer to "chill the (expletive) out." They arrested him for disorderly conduct.

Two days earlier, redshirt freshman defensive lineman Raymond Henderson made a snide comment to a woman and her adolescent daughter at a Knoxville restaurant. The details of Henderson's remark were unknown, but it was enough to get him kicked off the team. Fulmer also elected to suspend Mitchell indefinitely. Here we go again.

Screenwriter William Goldman wrote the line, mentioned earlier in this book, "Nobody knows anything." It still held true for the Vols. One player dismissed, another player arrested, and Gerald Riggs Jr. even showed up late to an interview with NFL personnel. Riggs, whose perpetual tardiness was one reason he spent most of his career at Tennessee pissing off the coaches and wasting away on the bench, showed up an hour late to his interviews with general managers, scouts and coaches in February at the NFL combine in Indianapolis, according to a source on an NFC team. The same Riggs who said that critics and coaches made too much of his immaturity issues; the same Riggs who said his problems were in the past and he was a different man; the same Riggs who said he would play in the NFL, essentially showed up an hour late for a job interview when injuries were already plummeting his draft stock. It was like struggling through school, still landing the job opportunity of a lifetime, then showing up late for the interview.

Riggs called it a "rumor" and said it started when he didn't show up for the bench press. "I wasn't doing the bench press," he said. "I wasn't supposed to be there."

Riggs was also battling, again, the presence of Fulmer. Riggs knew NFL teams would call Fulmer before the draft. Riggs also knew Fulmer might not give him the best recommendation. The two never formed a healthy relationship, and Fulmer couldn't forget those trying, infuriating first two years of Riggs' career.

"Gerald matured as a person, as a student and as a player," Fulmer said just before the 2006 NFL Draft, "though not to the degree I thought and wished he would have."

Responded Riggs, "It is what it is. I can't control what another man says. I really don't have a problem with the guy."

So the draft came and went, and Riggs, the can't-miss prospect coming out of high school, the darkhorse Heisman Trophy candidate, the 1,107-yard rusher, didn't hear his name. He wasn't drafted. Riggs watched the names of 255 other players—including fourteen running backs—appear on the television screen at his family's Atlanta home without ever seeing his own. The severe ankle injury he suffered against Alabama scared off most teams, and he accepted an undrafted free agent contract from the Miami Dolphins. You couldn't help but wonder how his tardiness in Indianapolis molded his perception among NFL personnel.

Nobody knows anything.

But Fulmer, the fifty-five-year-old dean of SEC coaches, was determined to learn and change like a wide-eyed rookie coach. Players said Fulmer completely lost his composure during the team meeting the night after Mitchell's arrest and had never seen him so upset. Fulmer released a fiery statement like you would see from New York Yankees owner George Steinbrenner following

Mitchell's arrest and Henderson's dismissal. He threatened to dismiss the next player who misbehaved.

And that's when the water bottles started flying.

The infamous Fulmer wince appeared one more time when I informed him that the details of his only unenjoyable season in his thirty-four years as a Tennessee player, assistant or head coach would be chronicled in a book. In a testament to the expectations facing Fulmer in 2005, this book was originally supposed to be about his run for a national title. That, well, didn't quite happen. But the wince turned into a shrug, and he never flinched throughout the rest of the conversation.

"Facts are facts," he said, offering a small smile.

Fulmer, despite all his miscues, excuses and deserved criticism, remained a man of integrity following the 2005 season. My newspaper, the *Chattanooga Times Free Press*, pays for a featured guest to speak at our Best of Preps banquet to honor the area's top high school athletes. Wildly popular men's basketball coach Bruce Pearl turned us down, so the newspaper immediately extended an offer to Fulmer. A previous engagement prevented Fulmer from accepting the offer, but he volunteered to hand-deliver a letter to offensive coordinator David Cutcliffe concerning details of the banquet. Fulmer promised to persuade Cutcliffe to make the speech, and not just because Steve Spurrier had spoken the year before.

Oh, and Fulmer's previous engagement? He was playing in a golf tournament in Nashville, Tenn., to raise money for The Jason Foundation, a group that works to raise awareness about teen suicide. Fulmer's longtime assistant, defensive end coach Steve Caldwell, had lost a son to suicide in 2002. Fulmer also graciously offered Rick Clausen, who had directed some dirty words toward his coach after the Florida game, a position on the offensive coaching staff as a graduate assistant. Clausen accepted.

Fulmer the person didn't change.

Fulmer the coach did change.

Fulmer, even after thirty-four years in the game, learned a lot about himself following the travails of the 2005 season. He had turned softer and mellower in his older age, sitting majestically atop the $2 million he made per season. Former Tennessee offensive lineman Bubba Miller, a star in the mid-1990s, once told me players sometimes despised Fulmer for his biting tongue and intense behavior on the practice field. Tell that to members of the 2005 team, and they would wonder if you're talking about the same person. The Vols, particularly on offense, behaved in practice as if a substitute teacher was in charge. Mistakes went unpunished, uncorrected and, as the season went on, unsolved. Fulmer remained loyal to assistants who were no longer effective in their jobs and protected players who caused distractions on and off the field.

Then 5–6 happened, Fulmer got knocked off his throne and, during the spring of 2006, acted like the "mean son of a bitch" Miller had described. The substitute teacher was gone.

The old teacher was back.

"Man, he's not letting anything slide this year," said defensive tackle Justin Harrell, and you start to understand what Bubba

Miller was talking about. "He's changed. He's not letting anything go."

He was no longer protecting his players. He was calling the weight of his offensive linemen "terrible" and also described young defensive tackle Demonte Bolden as "terrible" after one practice. He was chastising punter Britton Colquitt for missing a scrimmage, calling his excuse "lame." This is not the same Fulmer who suspended Tony McDaniel for a mere two games after rearranging a fellow student's face with a cheap shot.

"I'm telling them like I see it right now," Fulmer said. "I don't know if that's different, but maybe it is."

His demeanor resonated with the Vols. In 2005, bail bond representatives were scouting Tennessee more than the NFL. A week with just one arrest in spring of 2005 was a good week. The 2006 spring? Just one.

Too loyal? No one on the offensive side was coaching the same position they had the previous year. It was a complete overhaul. And instead of micromanaging the offense as he had the past few years, Fulmer was letting David Cutcliffe handle the offense just like John Chavis was handling the defense. It was just like 1998, when the Vols won a national title. "I think he's letting Coach Cutcliffe go a little bit and do his own thing," quarterback Erik Ainge said. "I think the biggest thing you see right now with Coach is he's sitting back a little bit and trusting everything is going to be fine with Coach Cut."

Fulmer's attitude was new yet old, familiar yet strange, and certainly one associated with a winner. Back when Miller and his teammates had grumbled in the dorm rooms about mean ol' Fulmer, their opponents were making similar complaints about them. The Vols had played with discipline, they'd been tough and, most importantly, they'd won.

"I know I've been a lot more vocal and a lot more aggressive," Fulmer said, "and back to myself, actually."

But the old Fulmer was still the competitive Fulmer, which meant the occasional excuse. Ridiculed by fans for his imaginative excuses during the 5–6 season, Fulmer started his spring 2006 press conference by dumping some blame on the players. Back in the fall, he'd pointed to a controversial chop-block call as one of the reasons Tennessee lost by thirteen to Georgia. (Even though the chop block forced Tennessee to punt, Georgia promptly threw an interception and Jonathan Wade returned it to the goal line.) Fulmer then blamed poor receiver play on injuries even though most of them never missed a game. He also blamed poor running on offensive line injuries even though Rob Smith, Albert Toeaina and Cody Douglas missed little time with injuries—and what football team goes through a season unscathed?—and pointed to a tough schedule for the 5–6 record.

While some of those excuses were bogus, no one denied that Tennessee had played a tough schedule in 2005. Fulmer's timing, however, could be considered questionable. During his post-game press conference following the loss to Vanderbilt—*freaking* Vanderbilt—Fulmer stated, "If the schedule was a little different, we might be 7–3 or something like that." And you might be able to picture how the Vols could be three games better if they had drawn Mississippi State and Arkansas out of the SEC West instead of LSU and Alabama, and hadn't scheduled Notre Dame. (But remember, if UAB's Lance Rhodes holds on to Darrell Hackney's fourth-quarter pass in the end zone and LSU doesn't suffer a complete meltdown, the Vols are easily 2–9. Breaks go both ways.)

But for Fulmer to make such a comment after losing to Vanderbilt at home made less sense than sticking with man coverage on Earl Bennett, and the message boards exploded with criticism. One columnist even suggested that Fulmer could use a public relations assistant. But 2006 was approaching, spring practice would soon begin, and Fulmer, while addressing the media, said, "I think we assumed too much as to where we were ability-wise."

And on that spring day, Dennis Dodd, the sharp, witty senior writer for CBS Sportsline, decided he had heard enough and blasted Fulmer for his comment.

"Anyone notice that Tennessee coach Phil Fulmer subtly threw his players under the bus this week?" Dodd wrote. "Phil is running out of excuses. He fired two offensive coaches. Offensive coordinator Randy Sanders quit under pressure. Quarterbacks were yo-yoed in and out of the lineup. Tennessee was a pre-season No. 3, so shame on all of us. That suggests the greatest over-evaluation of talent since Vanilla Ice. Tennessee lost its way, its soul and to Vandy, missing a bowl for the first time since 1988. To lay it on the players indicts the coaching staff for a) recruiting them and b) not developing the sub-standard talent (Fulmer's summation, not ours).

"If this is the way it's going be at Tennessee, the equipment managers better start watching their backs. They're next."

Fulmer bristled at the continued criticism during the spring. He could be heard echoing the sentiments of rocker Bob Seger, saying tersely he just wanted to "turn the page" at the mere mention of Tennessee's 5–6 season. "I'm ready to turn the page on 2005, and I think everyone has reviewed all they possibly can on the shortcomings of last year," Fulmer said.

Everyone except for Fulmer, who hadn't appeared to learn from all the distractions caused by problematic players in 2005. Offensive lineman Ell Ash, generally known as trouble before he began showing up at Daniel Brooks' patented brawls and getting kicked off the team for cursing out coaches, returned to practice March 30, 2006, for spring drills. He was back. And even though Fulmer admitted Ash had to convince some of the assistant coaches, whom he had chewed out the previous fall, to give him another chance, Fulmer was more than willing to let him back on the team. The decision bewildered Tennessee's beat reporters.

So much for turning the page.

"Some of the players on our unity council and some of our academic advisors approached me about giving him a second chance," Fulmer said. "Ell has convinced me he is serious about it. He has made apologies to the team and the appropriate coaches. He seems to have a very good attitude, but there are no promises."

Despite the occasional lapse, Fulmer stayed true to his word and became a tougher coach. By the end of spring, Fulmer went about telling fans on Tennessee's Big Orange Caravan Tour, where the coaches greet supporters around the Southeast, that coaching had played a role in the 5–6 season. He also finally admitted he'd completely butchered the quarterback situation. The Vols scored 205 points all season—they'd tallied 441 in 1998—and ranked 98th nationally in passing efficiency, just behind Louisiana-Monroe.

"Rick had played really well in the bowl game. We let them battle it out in the spring and summer," Fulmer recalled. "Rick actually played better, to a little bit of a degree, in two-a-days. Yet I had the decision to make with Florida, Georgia, Alabama, Notre Dame and LSU, in some order. I had to decide, could Rick beat those guys? Could we win as a team? I thought, the way Erik had played the year before, if he got reps early, he'd take off. As it turned out, I probably screwed both of them."

Ainge, who'd offered to take on a leadership role and begin accepting responsibility for the team's struggles following the departure of Rick Clausen, claimed that in September a turf toe injury was slowing him down considerably and that Tennessee's playbook looked like the Chinese alphabet. But Ainge didn't tell anyone because Fulmer's ill-fated quarterback competition seemed destined to last the entire season, and he didn't want to lose his job to Clausen on the practice field.

He would rather have taken his chances during the actual games. Ainge essentially admitted he put himself before the team, and, privately, a few teammates fumed. "Should I have said something? Yeah, but you never know if I wouldn't have played at all," Ainge said. "It's not like I could take two or three days off in a week and then try to play on Saturday. Every day at practice was a competition with me and Rick.

"Whether it was me not working hard enough or me having too much on me, whatever it was, it was just a little too much."

But Ainge, like Fulmer, was at least trying. He removed the diamond stud earrings that sparked some silly controversy among Tennessee fans on the message boards—Ainge's earrings did not cause him to heave floaters into triple coverage—and started participating in early-morning runs with his teammates. He became the shadow of new offensive coordinator and quarterbacks coach David Cutcliffe, who also received a rude awakening when he familiarized himself with the offense.

Or, rather, wondered what the hell happened to it after he had left in 1998. It wasn't familiar at all.

Yes, one more aspect of Tennessee football remained unchanged since the fall: the offense stunk, and Cutcliffe knew it. He grumbled about the weight of his receivers and offensive linemen, bemoaned the undisciplined nature of the offense and slow tempo of practice. Cutcliffe, so meticulous in his work, grew noticeably frustrated during spring practice. The dropped balls—there were thirty-three of those in the first practice—bad routes, poor decisions and busted plays irritated him so much that you wondered if a coach fresh off triple bypass heart surgery should even be allowed within a hundred yards of Tennessee's offense. Cutcliffe started arriving to work at 4:45 a.m.

in order to give himself enough time to solve Tennessee's woes offensively.

"It's the energy in practice," he said. "Football is like any sport. There's an energy that's critical. You didn't sense it. I'm not pointing fingers at anybody. I want that to be perfectly clear. You just didn't sense it."

So he started Camp Cutcliffe. He gave offensive players assigned seats in meetings. They couldn't slouch in their chairs, and they weren't allowed to wear a hat. He instructed the quarterbacks on how to take notes the proper way and even taught them the history of certain defensive alignments. Receivers started digging for pennies in five-gallon buckets of rice to improve hand strength and began catching bricks instead of footballs. But not even Cutcliffe, the intelligent, details-obsessed master of the offense could figure this bunch out.

During the first scrimmage, the offense still stunk.

"It was embarrassing to watch," Fulmer said after the Vols gave up ten sacks.

Halfway through spring practice, the offense still stunk.

"I don't think anyone should be just real thrilled right now about the offense," Fulmer said. "It's not what the defense is doing. It's what the offense isn't doing."

As I write this, almost at the end of spring practice in 2006, the first-down marker still looks about 50 yards away to Tennessee's offense. Receiver Jayson Swain's knee is hurting. Running backs Arian Foster and LaMarcus Coker are coming off surgery. And the highlight of spring practice for the offense was the play of basketball forward Stanley Asumnu, who put on a helmet for the first time since eighth grade and made the lone big catch of Tennessee's next-to-last scrimmage. After the scrimmage, Asumnu admitted he had no idea what he was doing out there. So what does that say for the rest of them?

"The only exciting thing that happened, and it was Stanley who did it," Fulmer said, the frustration evident in his voice.

But give Tennessee fans credit. Their expectations are outlandish, their reactions are extreme, their criticism is, at times, unreasonable. There's a reason Neyland Stadium seats 107,000 on Saturdays during the fall and the basketball arena can hold 25,000. Tennessee fans always believe. According to one UT official, the athletic department raised more money in December than ever before, blew away its typical January and February earnings and sold almost every club seat for the renovated Neyland Stadium. Despite an incredibly questionable offense and all those defections on defense, no one is conceding 2006 to Georgia or Florida or especially South Carolina. The passion of Vols fans never subsides. They believe in Fulmer. They believe in Chavis. They believe in Cutcliffe, and, gosh, if you believe in Cutcliffe, then you have to believe in the players on offense.

Sure, given the offense's woes, Ash's return and Ainge's stab at leadership, it seems someone could write the same type of book all over again in the 2006 season. Nobody knows anything, the saying goes, and it also includes the media. We were the ones hyping Tennessee as national championship contenders. We were wrong.

But who knows? Maybe Ainge will play like he did as a freshman and the defense, as usual, won't slow down a bit under Chavis. Maybe the Vols will look just like they did when Cutcliffe was last seen around here back in 1998, the last time they won a national or conference championship. One fact is certain: Neyland Stadium will always be full of believers, and on opening kickoff, a 5-6 season will once again seem ridiculous and a SEC championship will not.

Only then will the memories of 2005 start to fade.